DEAL
WITH IT!

WORKBOOK

YOU CANNOT CONQUER WHAT

YOU WILL NOT CONFRONT

PAULA WHITE

D1361152

NELSON REFERENCE & ELECTRONIC
A Division of Thomas Nelson Publishers
Since 1798

www.thomasnelson.com

Published in Nashville, Tennessee, by Thomas Nelson, Inc.

Unless otherwise indicated, Scripture quotations are from the New King James Version® (NKJV), copyright © 1979, 1980, 1982, 1992 by Thomas Nelson, Inc. Used by permission. All rights reserved.

Scripture quotations marked KJV are taken from *The Holy Bible*, King James Version.

ISBN: 1-4185-0125-5

Printed in the United States of America

06 07 08 09 VG 9 8 7 6 5 4 3 2

First and foremost, thank You, Lord, for Your unfailing love and Your greatness. You are amazing! Words will never articulate my love and desire for You.

To my husband, my coach, my best friend and covenant partner, Randy, who encourages and inspires me to be all that God has destined for me. You are a rare gem that becomes more valuable each day. My love for you is indescribable.

To my four children—Bradley, Brandon, Angie and Kristen. You are my joy and motivation. You have my heart! I believe in you and am so proud of you.

To my spiritual father and mother, Bishop T. D. and First Lady Serita Jakes. Your wisdom and guidance have been invaluable and have helped mold me and navigate the destiny of my life. I honor you and love you.

To the staff of Paula White Ministries and Without Walls International Church. Thank you for faithfully serving the Lord and your diligence to bring the vision to pass. Great will be your reward.

To my extended family and friends, whom I love and appreciate.

And to my World Partners. Without you, Paula White Ministries would not be what it is today. Thank you for believing in a "messed up Mississippi girl" with a big God and a big dream. Together we are transforming lives, healing hearts and saving souls.

CONTENTS

INTRODUCTION:
CONFRONTATION LEADS TO CONQUEST

Hebrews 4:12 teaches us that the Word of God is "living and powerful, and sharper than any two-edged sword, piercing even to the division of soul and spirit, and of joints and marrow, and is a discerner of the thoughts and intents of the heart." Practically speaking, that means that God's holy Word helps us recognize our sins, our shortcomings, our failures, and our faults.

The Word makes us aware of these things not so that we will feel condemned, but so that we can repent, receive forgiveness and be released into all the freedom and fullness God has for us. His desire is to mold us into people who reflect Jesus in our character, in our attitudes, in our thoughts, in our words and in our actions. He wants the life and passion of Jesus to course through us and empower us—and to flow through us to bless others. If we are going to live that way, we must identify, confront, and conquer the issues that keep us from having God's best in our lives. When we truly deal with these things, God will heal us, restore us, set us free, and lead us into the great destiny He has for us and we will live joyful, purposeful, totally fulfilling lives.

Personally, I have had to deal with many things. I tell my story in greater detail in the book *Deal With It!* but for now, let me just say that some of my issues were messes of my own making and some were the results of tragedies and trauma that were not my fault. Regardless, I reached a point at which I had to face it head-on if I wanted to live the wonderful life God wanted for me.

When I determined to deal with my issues, I picked up my Bible, held it up to the Lord and said, "Lord, I don't want to be going around this mountain when I'm forty or fifty years old. I don't want to be struggling with the same issues and hurts deep in my soul. Help me!"

I began to study my Bible diligently and to examine especially the women of the Bible. They became my mentors as I realized they had also faced very serious issues in their lives and discovered some crucial success principles and simple, yet profound answers.

What I learned from them, I trust you will also learn from them. I write more thoroughly about the lessons these women taught me in the book, *Deal With It!* I urge you to read that book and to have it handy, along with your Bible, as you go through this workbook. You can use the workbook without the book if you have a strong biblical background that includes knowing the stories of these women well, but to get the most out of the workbook and thoroughly learn its lessons, you will benefit greatly from reading the book.

I have developed this workbook as a companion to the book, *Deal With It!* Here, we will focus on the key points in the book in such a way that you can begin to apply the major lessons from these women to your own life. You will have opportunities to identify and begin to deal with your issues here in the privacy of these pages as you answer the questions I ask. You will be enriched as you "work the Word" by reading the suggested Bible verses, writing down what they mean to you, and applying them to your life.

I know with all my heart that God wants to help you deal with the things that are holding you back. But I also know that He will not do it for you. This workbook is based on a premise I learned years ago: *You can't conquer what you will not confront.* And you can't confront what is not identified. God will reveal the issues that need to be dealt with in you; He will give you glimpses of the destiny He has for you; He will encourage and assist as you confront the obstacles in your life—but He will not face them for you. You must deal with your issues yourself.

I want to challenge you today to deal with everything you need to deal with. I challenge you to go after all that God has for you. I challenge you to apprehend every blessing, to attain your wildest dreams, and to embrace the destiny He wants to unfold before you. I challenge you to face the facts about your life, your past, the condition of your heart, your attitudes and mindsets, and your behavior because I know that once you face the facts and identify your issues, you can deal with them. When you deal with them, you can defeat them and walk in greater victory than you have ever known. So come on, get ready to turn the page and get started. God is for you; He will help you and lead you as you deal with it!

As you walk through this study, carefully look at the ten women God used to unveil His plan, and realize that no matter who you are, He has plans for you in His Kingdom. But before He can use you to the fullest extent, you must rid yourself of the thoughts and behaviors that hold you back—and whatever those thoughts and behaviors are, it's time to deal with it! It is my prayer that you will find new meaning for your life as you walk through the timeless lessons in this workbook.

Lesson 1

RUTH:
Dealing with Your Past

To understand who Ruth was and the challenges she faced, please read Ruth 1:16–22 and Chapter 1 of the book, *Deal With It!*

DAY 1: RISE ABOVE YOUR PAST

Even though her past was filled with idol worship, the perversion of her culture, disappointment and death, there was something great about Ruth. She rose above her past. When presented with the opportunity to accompany Naomi to Bethlehem and begin a new life there, Ruth said, basically, "I want no more of this. I want something better. I want something more." Even when Naomi urged her to return to Moab, thinking her chances of remarriage would be better there, Ruth responded, "Your people shall be my people, and your God, my God" (Ruth 1:16, NKJV). Ruth wanted Naomi's customs, Naomi's traditions, and Naomi's God. She was saying to her, "I'm going where I've never been to create something I've never had . . . because in knowing you, Naomi, I've come to love you. I've come to know your God and love your God. I'm willing to go where I have never been to become something I want to be."

Millions of people today—maybe even you—are where Ruth was in that moment. If so, I urge you today to deal with your past. Let go of old grudges; release your old anger and disappointments; and ask God to heal you of old hurts. Determine to learn to make new choices, to embrace the Word of God as your guidebook for life and to let the Holy Spirit lead you in every decision you make, every day of your life.

You cannot embrace tomorrow if you cling to your past. You *must* let go. This is often easier said than done because the past is familiar and because a sense of security does come with clinging to the familiar—even if the familiar is bad.

I proclaim to you that your tomorrow does not have to be like your yesterday. God has great and wonderful things ahead for you, and He will give you the strength to let go of your past and rise above it so you can fully enter into the days to come.

CONFRONT

1. In what ways have you allowed your past to determine your present?

   _____

   _____

   _____

   _____

2. In what ways do you think your past could influence your future if you do not deal with it? _____

   _____

   _____

   _____

   _____

3. What specific decisions do you need to make and actions do you need to take in order to rise above your past?

   _____

   _____

   _____

   _____

CONQUER

What do the Scriptures below mean to you personally and how can you apply them in your life?

Isaiah 42:9 _____

_____

_____

_____

Isaiah 43:18, 19 _____

_____

_____

_____

Revelation 21:4 _____

_____

_____

_____

DAY 2: WALK TOWARD BETHLEHEM

Just as we arrive at a natural destination by taking one step at a time, arriving at the future God has for us is also a continual process. We cannot simply "cut off" the past in an instant; we have to walk out of it little by little. Let me share with you five things to consider as you leave your past and head into your future:

1. *God does not consult your past to determine your future.* He does not look at or consider your past when He thinks about your future—and you don't have to either!

2. *God commands you to leave your past and press toward the future He has for you.* You must let go of the past, forget the things that are behind you, reach forward to what is before you, and resist everything that hinders your pursuit of destiny.

3. *God* always *has a future for you.* Ruth had no hope of marriage and children in following Naomi to Bethlehem. Nevertheless, she chose to walk toward

Bethlehem—the place of hope, provision, redemption, and joy. In that new place, God blessed her abundantly.

4. *Change your focus.* Begin to see yourself in new ways and to think new thoughts. Take your focus off the negative things that have happened and put your focus on the *good* things God has done, is doing, and will do for you.

5. *Prepare yourself in the Word.* Begin to prepare yourself for what is coming. Believe and obey God's Word as you "walk toward Bethlehem," fully embracing your wonderful future.

I don't know what your Moab is, but we all have something we must leave if we are to follow Jesus completely. I don't know where your Bethlehem is or who your Boaz is, but God has a place and a purpose for you if you are willing to leave your past and walk into your future with Him.

CONFRONT

1. Today, how can you take one small step away from the past you want to leave behind? _____

   _____

   _____

   _____

2. What do you need to *stop* focusing on and what do you need to *start* focusing on in order to set your gaze on the good things God has for you in the future? _____

   _____

   _____

   _____

3. What specific Scripture(s) will you use to prepare yourself to walk into your future? Choose some of your own and write them in the space provided or use the ones listed in "Work the Word" below.

   _____

_____

_____

_____

CONQUER

What do the Scriptures below mean to you personally and how can you apply them in your life?

Luke 9:62 _____

_____

_____

_____

Proverbs 4:25 _____

_____

_____

_____

Philippians 3:13, 14 _____

_____

_____

_____

DAY 3: GOD FORGIVES AND FORGETS

Second Corinthians 5:17 declares, "Therefore, if anyone is in Christ, he is a new creation; old things have passed away; behold, all things have become new" (NKJV).

This verse means that the moment you came to Jesus, everything "old" passed away from your life, and you became a new person through Christ Jesus. Your sins were not only forgiven, but even better, it is as though you *never* committed them in the eyes of God. He not only forgave you; He totally forgot about your past. It was truly behind you, and you were cleansed and made new. God's Word says:

> He has not dealt with us according to our sins,
> Nor punished us according to our iniquities.
> For as the heavens are high above the earth,
> So great is His mercy toward those who fear Him;
> As far as the east is from the west,
> So far has He removed our transgressions from us. (Ps. 103:10–12, NKJV)

God has no trouble believing the miracle He works in our lives when He forgives us and removes our sin "as far as the east is from the west." *We* are the ones who have trouble believing we are forgiven. *We* are the ones who have trouble letting go of the past. *We* are the ones who keep reminding ourselves of our past sin and shame. *We* are the ones who refuse to walk out of Moab and take the journey to Bethlehem.

I believe God is saying to you today that He has something for you that is greater, healthier, better, finer, holier, and more beautiful than you have ever seen or experienced. I urge you to hear His voice and pursue His vision for your life. It will lead you into a "land flowing with milk and honey," a place of peace and prosperity. You can do it; you have been made new.

CONFRONT

1. Describe what it means to you personally that God says you are a "new creation." _____

   _____

   _____

   _____

   _____

2. Have you fully accepted God's forgiveness for your sins? If not, pray and thank Him for sending Jesus to die on the Cross for your sins and tell Him that you receive the forgiveness Jesus purchased for you.

   _____

   _____

_____

_____

3. What practical steps can you take or new choices can you make to
   indicate your belief in God's ability to make you new? _____

   _____

   _____

   _____

CONQUER

What do the Scriptures below mean to you personally and how can you
apply them in your life?

Hebrews 8:12 _____

_____

_____

_____

Ephesians 1:7 _____

_____

_____

_____

1 John 1:9 _____

_____

_____

_____

DAY 4: KEEP ON KEEPING ON

Ruth did not move into her destiny overnight. Instead, she continually demon-
strated three qualities that were vital to receiving the fullness of God's great purpose for her life.

1. *Ongoing Work and Productivity.* Ruth did not show up in Bethlehem and expect her destiny to be handed to her on a silver platter. No, she went into the barley harvest, got busy, and labored tirelessly—and as she was *working*, Boaz noticed her.

You became a new creation the moment you accepted Jesus as your Savior, but you are responsible to *walk* out and to *work* out the newness of life He gives you. If you want to live a successful Christian life, you need to work at it!

2. *An Ongoing Obsession with Doing Good.* God positions us for promotion as we work and seek to do good to others. Ruth may have appeared to be a lowly laborer as she gleaned, but she was in precisely the *right* position to be raised up by the Lord! She put in long hours of dirty, hard physical labor because she was determined to serve and care for Naomi. Ruth learned that no job is too little or too "unimportant" if we are seeking to serve others and that every person is worthy of our best.

3. *An Ongoing Following of Instructions.* By listening closely and following the instructions of those in authority, we give them honor, and as we honor them, we honor the Lord who is over them.

Ruth listened to Naomi and heeded her advice when Naomi taught her how to speak to Boaz. She listened to Boaz as he told her how and where to collect the grain she needed. As she obeyed those in authority, she found herself positioned for great blessing and promotion.

The same God who sees your ongoing work and productivity, your desire to do good, and your ongoing willingness to honor those in authority, is the God who has already prepared a reward for you.

CONFRONT

1. How is your work ethic? In what ways do you need to be more diligent or increase your productivity? _____

   _____

   _____

   _____

   _____

2. Are you obsessed with doing good? How can you better serve those around you? _____

_____

_____

_____

_____

3. Who has God put in authority over you? How can you better receive and obey the godly, life-giving instructions these people offer you?

_____

_____

_____

_____

CONQUER

What do the Scriptures below mean to you personally and how can you apply them in your life?

1 Corinthians 15:58 _____

_____

_____

_____

2 Thessalonians 3:13 _____

_____

_____

_____

Hebrews 13:17 _____

_____

_____

_____

DAY 5: ENTERING INTO GOD'S DESTINY

What was God's plan and purpose for Ruth? Her destiny included becoming the wife of Boaz and the mother of a baby named Obed. This baby grew up to become the great-grandfather of David, an ancestor of Jesus Christ. Ruth's destiny was to be part of the royal bloodline of our Savior and Lord!

When God desires to bring change on a large scale, He uses someone who has been changed. That certainly was the case in Ruth's life. God changed her, and she changed history.

You also have the capacity to bring God's desired changes to the world around you, whether that world is your family, your church, your city, your nation, or all of planet Earth. God has placed a dream and a destiny within you; His heart is full of plans and purposes for you to accomplish. You are carrying within you the seed of "something new." But to usher in that something new, you must leave the old things behind.

Ruth was a heathen-born woman from a country that murdered babies. Yet she changed and became the ancestor of Jesus, who died to give "born-again" life to the heathen!

Ruth—who was marred, scarred, stained, tainted, distorted, and warped by her early environment—lived out her life in greatness. What God did in Ruth's life, He can do in yours.

I urge you to disconnect from your past and move toward the presence of greatness in your future. Trust God and allow Him to do His work of change and preparation in you. Get to the place in your life where you look yourself in the mirror and say:

"I am not a product of my past."

"I am not a product of my environment."

"I am not who other people say that I am."

"I am who God says I am."

"I am who God is calling me to be."

"I am willing to move into the destiny God has prepared for me and that He is preparing me to fulfill."

I assure you that a person with your kind of past can succeed, can be used by God, can fulfill all of His plans and purposes. You can succeed. You can have a future that is blessed and fulfilling and eternally rewarding.

Deal with every past thing that seeks to hold you back from your future. Ask God today to help you leave your past behind and to embrace all that He has for you.

CONFRONT

1. How is God changing you right now? _____

   _____

   _____

   _____

   _____

2. Do you believe there is greatness in you? If so, how would you describe it? If not, pray and ask God to reveal it to you. _____

   _____

   _____

   _____

   _____

3. Are you willing to move into the destiny God has prepared for you and that He is preparing you to fulfill? _____

   _____

   _____

   _____

   _____

CONQUER

What do the Scriptures below mean to you personally and how can you apply them in your life?

Jeremiah 29:11 _____

_____

_____

_____

Jeremiah 17:7 _____

_____

_____

_____

Philippians 4:13 _____

_____

_____

_____

Lesson 2

LEAH:
DEALING WITH YOURSELF

To understand who Leah was and the challenges she faced, read Genesis 29:15–35 and Chapter 2 of the book, *Deal With It!*

DAY 1: SEE ME, HEAR ME, KNOW ME, PRAISE GOD

I am fascinated by the names of Jacob and Leah's first four sons. Those names reveal the silent cries of Leah's heart as she sought to accept herself and win the acceptance of her husband.

See Me! Leah named her firstborn son Reuben, which means "look at me."

When a woman is totally ignored by a man with whom she desires to have a loving relationship, her heart is crushed and her self-esteem shattered. Because she begins to think something is wrong with her, she often tries to prove her value in other ways.

Hear Me! Leah had a second son named Simeon, which means "to hear." In naming him, Leah was crying out to Jacob, "Listen to me!" She was begging to have her opinions, her feelings, and her desires heard. When a woman is ignored, her feelings of self-worth are destroyed.

Know Me! Leah's third son was named Levi, which means to "be joined to or connected with." Levi's name reveals Leah's deep desire for intimacy with her husband. Having children with a man is no guarantee that he will see, hear, or be intimate with the woman who longs for intimacy with him. After Levi's birth, Leah finally said to herself, *I can't get his attention. He won't listen to me. He won't be one with me. It's time to change direction.*

Praise God! Leah then gave birth to her fourth son, Judah, which means "let Jehovah be praised!"

Tremendous freedom and security result when we turn from seeking the attention of people and focus on praising the Lord. The more we praise Him, the less concerned we become about whether others see us, listen to us, or value us.

Until you personally bring forth the name of Judah, you will always need people to fulfill you, see you, hear you, and be intimate with you. Once you become totally devoted to praise, you will be able to look to God alone for validation. The greatest way to find acceptance and fulfillment in life is to praise God!

CONFRONT

1. In what ways have you expressed your longing for others to "see me," "hear me," and "know me"? _____

_____

_____

_____

_____

2. What was the turning point at which you finally learned to praise God? If you have not reached that point yet, pray and ask God to help you. _____

_____

_____

_____

_____

3. What benefit and blessing does praising God bring into your life?

_____

_____

_____

_____

CONQUER

What do the Scriptures below mean to you personally and how can you apply them in your life?

Psalm 34:1 _____

_____

_____

_____

Psalm 63:3 _____

_____

_____

_____

Hebrews 13:15 _____

_____

_____

_____

DAY 2: EXPERIENCE GOD'S LOVE PERSONALLY

Many people have heard that God loves them. A well-known Bible verse says, "For God so loved the world that He gave His only begotten Son, that whoever believes in Him should not perish but have everlasting life" (John 3:16). However, "head knowledge" that God loves us is not the same as knowing His love personally and experientially. To really know the love of God is to be convinced of it in your entire being on a deep and intimate level, not just in your mind.

How do you receive an experiential "knowing" of God's love? By entering into the presence of God. And how do you do that? By praising and worshiping Him. Praise ushers us into God's very presence, and the more we praise Him, the more we begin to see ourselves as God sees us and to understand His purpose for our lives.

If you haven't experienced loving relationships with people, it is even more important to stay in the presence of God. In His presence, you will desire and risk *receiving* God's love. In His presence, you will begin to understand all that He has placed inside you, all that He desires to give you, all that He declares is yours as His beloved child and heir. In His presence, your problems are "no problem" because God is your loving Father who will provide for you and protect you.

In God's presence, you will be empowered to love yourself—to accept yourself as His specially-created, beloved child. You will also begin to believe in God's purpose for your life, to acknowledge the gifts He has imparted, and to have the courage to step into everything He has destined for you.

CONFRONT

1. In your own words, describe your experience with God's love.

   _____

   _____

   _____

   _____

2. What happens to you personally when you are in God's presence?

   _____

   _____

   _____

   _____

3. How has God's love given you strength and courage in the past? Can you believe in Him to give you strength and courage to pursue your destiny now and in the future? _____

   _____

   _____

   _____

   _____

CONQUER

What do the Scriptures below mean to you personally and how can you apply them in your life?

Isaiah 43:4 _____

_____

_____

_____

Jeremiah 31:3 _____

_____

_____

_____

1 John 3:1 _____

_____

_____

_____

DAY 3: EXAMINE YOUR RELATIONSHIPS

Part of valuing yourself means refusing to be enmeshed in unhealthy relationships. What is an unhealthy relationship? Here are three major indicators:

- *Constant Strife and Division.* First, there will be constant strife and division that saps energy, sucks out joy, drains creativity, and distracts you from God's call. James 3:16 says, "For where envy and self-seeking exist, confusion and every evil thing are there" (NKJV). On the contrary, a healthy relationship includes a unity of purpose, values, and beliefs.

- *People Who Knew You "Back When."* Some of the most dangerous relationships are those that bind you to your past. Past associations can drag you down and keep you from fulfilling your potential.

Of course, you can't simply walk away from a parent, spouse, sibling, or child. But you can distance yourself from those "non-covenantal" or casual relationships that continually remind you of what people *used* to think of you. Their old opinions are not God's opinions. They do not relate to your tomorrows; they only relate to your yesterdays.

- *Violators of the Heart.* These are controlling people who prey on a person's heart. Violators take advantage of the "needs" in your life, especially your need to be loved and accepted. They aren't concerned about your blessings or your destiny. They are concerned only about what they want.

The most dangerous violator of the heart is the person who tells you what you want to hear, someone who insincerely strokes your ego and speaks words of affection you are desperate to hear—all in an effort to get what *they* want from you.

Evaluate your relationships and determine whether they deplete and control you or whether they are life-giving and mutually affirming. A healthy relationship includes balance between giving and taking, mutual appreciation and encouragement, and honest words of appreciation without any taint of manipulation.

CONFRONT

1. Are you entangled in any relationships that involve constant strife and division? If so, what will you do about them? _____
   _____
   _____
   _____
   _____

2. Are there any past associations you need to cut off from your life? If so, what will you do about them? _____

_____

_____

_____

_____

3. Are you in relationship with any violators of your heart? If so, what will you do about them?

_____

_____

_____

_____

_____

CONQUER

What do the Scriptures below mean to you personally and how can you apply them in your life?

Ephesians 4:1–3 _____

_____

_____

_____

Romans 16:17 _____

_____

_____

_____

1 Thessalonians 5:11 _____

_____

_____

_____

DAY 4: HOW TO LEAVE AN
UNHEALTHY RELATIONSHIP

How do you walk away from unhealthy relationships so that you can walk into the great life God has for you?

First, identify and accept the reality of out-of-balance relationships. At times, you need to take stock of an unhealthy situation and admit to yourself that the relationship just isn't working. If all efforts to bring the relationship into balance have failed, give that person "over" to God. Giving people over to God means releasing them to the One who truly can heal them, will never fail them, and is totally qualified to counsel and guide them.

Second, don't try to be God to another person. There's a huge difference between helping a person and carrying a person. You aren't the Holy Spirit. Do not prolong an enabling relationship in which you feel totally responsible for someone's success or failure.

Third, become comfortable with criticism. Everyone will not be happy with a decision to end a relationship. There will always to be someone who wants you to do something other than what God is leading you to do.

It's important to trust God to help you recognize when a relationship is becoming harmful. Trust Him to give you the courage to end the relationship and then give you thick enough skin to take the criticism that may come.

Fourth, end unhealthy relationships progressively. Ending unhealthy relationships requires emotional energy, and ending them all at once is likely to be overwhelming. Eliminate unhealthy relationships one at a time until all your relationships are pleasing to God and involve mutual give-and-take, mutual blessing, and mutual edification.

Fifth, don't burn bridges. If it is necessary to dissolve a relationship, don't do so in anger or bitterness. Be kind, but firm. Be compassionate, but determined to do what is right for you. Make a clean, definitive break. And then, move forward. Jesus said, "No one, having put his hand to the plow, and looking back, is fit for the kingdom of God" (Luke 9:62, NKJV). The word *fit* means "qualified for authority." If we continue to look back, we won't be qualified or given the authority to possess what God has for us. Look ahead and walk that way.

CONFRONT

1. Is there anyone in your life that you need to "give over" to God? How will you release that person to Him? _____

_____

_____

_____

_____

2. How will you handle the criticism you may face as you end certain relationships? _____

_____

_____

_____

_____

3. Given your personality and way of doing things, what will be the best way for you to go about ending an unhealthy relationship without burning bridges? _____

_____

_____

_____

_____

CONQUER

What do the Scriptures below mean to you personally and how can you apply them in your life?

1 Corinthians 15:33 _____

_____

_____

_____

Proverbs 27:6 _____

_____

_____

_____

Hebrews 12:1 _____

_____

_____

_____

DAY 5: HOW TO BUILD GOOD RELATIONSHIPS

The best way to start building a good relationship is to form partnerships and associations based upon two things: a common direction and the same destination.

- *A Common Direction.* We need to be in relationship with people whose lives are moving in the same direction as ours—people who have common vision, values, and goals. Without a common direction, there will be continual conflict.

Marriages, families, ministries, businesses, churches, and friendships all need unity. They need to be based on the things we have in common, the things that make us one and bring unity. Things like a passionate love for God, dedication to follow where He leads, determination to live by His Word, devotion to His people, and desire for His purposes to come to pass in every area of our lives.

- *The Same Destination.* To have the same destination is to have a conscious commitment to a common goal.

God tells us very clearly that He has a *deliberate destination* or an *expected end* for us as His children. Jeremiah 29:11 declares: "For I know the thoughts that

I think toward you, saith the LORD, thoughts of peace, and not of evil, to give you an expected end" (KJV). God has an expected end for you—a destiny He wants you to fulfill and a place He wants you to be when all is said and done. Make sure those who walk with you are heading toward that same destination, that they too are pursuing God's plans and purposes for their lives, and that they are as committed as you are to reaching God's expected end.

CONFRONT

1. Are you and your friends going in a common direction in life? What is that common direction?

   _____

   _____

   _____

   _____

   _____

2. Do you and your friends have the same destination? How would you describe it?

   _____

   _____

   _____

   _____

   _____

3. Are you helping others, and are they helping you to "come to the unity of the faith and of the knowledge of the Son of God" (Eph. 4:13)?

   _____

   _____

   _____

   _____

CONQUER

What do the Scriptures below mean to you personally and how can you apply them in your life?

Ephesians 4:3–6 _____

_____

_____

_____

Amos 3:3 _____

_____

_____

_____

Psalm 133:1–3 _____

_____

_____

_____

Lesson 3

RAHAB:
Dealing with Change

To understand who Rahab was and the challenges she faced, read Joshua 2:1–21 and Chapter 3 of the book, *Deal With It!*

DAY 1: BE SUCCESSFUL ON THE INSIDE

The biblical account of Rahab indicates that she enjoyed a tremendous amount of public success, but was empty on the inside. Today, we see people with worldly success, beauty, fame, money, even well-known ministries, and we think they have "arrived." The truth is that everyone, regardless of the way things appear, needs Jesus. Without Him, we are all empty, restless, unstable, and unsure about our purpose in life. He wants to bring change to our lives so that we can align with His purposes, walk in the destiny He has for us, and be filled to overflowing with His joy, His peace, and His love.

In order to embrace the changes God wants to bring in your life, start by examining yourself on the inside—your attitudes, your motives, your unresolved issues. As you examine yourself within, you will begin to see glimpses of the greatness God has deposited in you. You will begin to see yourself as a treasure chest filled with possibilities and you will begin to long for God to change you as He sees fit so that He can turn your possibilities into realities.

The enemy doesn't want you to birth the promises of God that are within you and he will oppose you when you begin to do so. When he does, cling to the truth that God has called you with an *eternal* purpose. Where you are right now, is not where you are going to be. God has an appointed task for you. He is doing an awesome work in you. He is the Author of the work in you, and He is the One who will finish it.

CONFRONT

1. Have you told Jesus lately how much you need Him? If not, recommit yourself to Him right now and ask Him to bring about the changes He wants to bring in your life. _____

_____

_____

_____

_____

2. As you examine yourself on the inside, what areas of your life do you think most need God's life-changing touch? _____

_____

_____

_____

_____

3. Can you identify anything in your life right now that the enemy may be using to keep you from embracing the changes God wants to bring to you? _____

_____

_____

_____

_____

CONQUER

What do the Scriptures below mean to you personally and how can you apply them in your life?

Romans 3:23 _____

_____

_____

_____

Philippians 1:6 _____

_____

_____

_____

Hebrews 12:2 _____

_____

_____

_____

DAY 2: COOPERATE WITH CHANGE

Rahab's story teaches four biblical truths that will help you cooperate with the changes God wants to bring to your life, if you will remember and abide by them.

First, God hears the heart's cry of every person who calls out to Him as Lord. God does not discriminate on the basis of gender, age, education, or economic status. If you believe in God and cry out for His help with a sincere heart, He *will* hear you.

Second, God does not determine the promise of our future by looking at our past. Regardless of where you have been or what you have done in your miserable, messed-up past, all of God's promises are available to you the moment you cry out to Him. Acts 10:34, 35 asserts, "God shows no partiality. But in every nation whoever fears him and works righteousness is accepted by Him" (NKJV).

Third, God honors faith. Faith in God is what brings His promises to pass. He doesn't look at your resumé; He says, "If you will give Me your faith, I will give you your future." God doesn't help you or raise you up because of what you do or don't do. He raises you up because you have faith in the finished work of Christ Jesus on the Cross. God does miracles for anyone who trusts Him completely. Faith is an equal-opportunity business!

Faith must be activated. Your faith empowers you to attain all that the Father has promised. But, it must be *activated*. To activate your faith, step out on God's Word and obey it. When you read or remember a Bible verse or a biblical principle, then simply do what it says to do. As you activate your faith in that way, God's promises begin to manifest in your life.

CONFRONT

1. Have you been guilty of thinking God would not hear you if you cried out to Him? Try again right now and pour out your heart to Him. I promise, He'll hear! _____

_____

_____

_____

_____

2. Briefly describe what it means for you personally to have faith in Jesus' finished work on the Cross. _____

_____

_____

_____

_____

3. In what practical ways can you activate your faith today? _____

_____

_____

_____

_____

CONQUER

What do the Scriptures below mean to you personally and how can you apply them in your life?

Psalm 34:17 _____

_____

_____

_____

2 Corinthians 5:7 _____

_____

_____

Hebrews 11:6 _____

_____

_____

DAY 3: CHOOSE THE BLESSING

Rahab received specific instructions from the spies to whom she had given shelter and to whom she offered a way of escape. She listened to these men and followed their instructions.

God's Word gives us instructions. His commands are laid out before us as a choice—we can *choose* whether we will obey or disobey. They are given for our blessing, so that we might live abundantly and possess all God has for us.

Our choices have consequences. If we choose not to obey God's instructions, we face the ramifications of our rebellion. We may not like those consequences, but we receive them nonetheless. We may not like the way God instructs us or sets up His system of commandments and statutes and judgments, but He has established the system for our good and He calls us to obey.

Similarly, the Israelite spies were clear with Rahab. They were willing to make an agreement with her: "Our lives for yours." But, they also made it clear that if she did not do precisely what they instructed her to do, they would not be responsible for her certain death. Rahab replied to them, "According to your words, so be it" (Josh. 2:21, NKJV). Rahab had a choice. She *chose* to follow the instructions given to her by the Israelite spies.

Likewise, God calls you to obedience. He desires obedience more than sacrifice (1 Sam. 15:22). In other words, God wants you to say "yes" to His commandments and instructions so that you will not sin, instead of finding yourself in need of forgiveness for having committed sin. If you will walk in obedience, you will avoid the consequences of disobedience and reap the rich rewards that come from following the God who loves you!

CONFRONT

1. Recall a time when you obeyed God. What blessings came from your obedience? _____

_____

_____

_____

2. Are you aware of any specific instructions from the Lord that you have not obeyed? Ask God to forgive your disobedience and help you to obey. _____

_____

_____

_____

3. What choices are before you right now? Ask God to help you choose well and obey Him so that you can enjoy the fullness and joy He has for you. _____

_____

_____

_____

Trinity Assembly of God

Women's Fellowship Presents:

"The Four S's"

What do they mean? Come join us and discover their meaning.

Invite a friend!

Where: Irma Salas
527A Sixth Ave
Brooklyn, NY 11215
718-788-3926

When: Saturday, January 20, 2007

Time: 11:30a.m.
Lunch and Transportation provided*

*Please note: For transportation we're meeting at 11:30am at:
Trinity Church
138 Henry Street
NY, NY 10002
212-267-1866

CONQUER

What do the Scriptures below mean to you personally and how can you apply them in your life?

Deuteronomy 30:15, 16 _____

_____

_____

_____

Deuteronomy 11:26–28 _____

_____

_____

_____

Romans 6:16 _____

_____

_____

_____

DAY 4: REMEMBER THE BLOOD

The scarlet cord in Rahab's window represented the blood covenant God had made with His people many years before, on the night He delivered them from Egypt. He had instructed them to put blood on their doorposts and lintels to keep the destroyer from bringing death to their households. Likewise, the scarlet cord in Rahab's window said clearly to the invading Isrealite army: *"Do not destroy this house."*

God sends a similar message to the enemy of your soul when you apply the shed blood of Jesus to your life. The devil has no legal right or authority to cross the "bloodline."

The blood of Jesus makes atonement for your sin; it ensures your total forgiveness (Lev. 17:11). It also redeems, cleanses, and purifies you (1 Pet. 1:18, 19; Heb. 9:14; Rev. 1:5, 6). Because of Jesus' shed blood you can *live*—not only an abundant life now, but an eternal life; not only a righteous life now, but a glorious life forever; not only a purified past, but a rewarding, blessed, fulfilling life throughout the endless ages to come.

Rahab "bound the scarlet cord in the window" (Josh. 2:21, NKJV). To *bind* is to attach, to fix, to tie in a way that cannot be untied. I encourage you to bind yourself to Christ Jesus in such a way that no person, experience, or force can "undo" you. As the Lord changes you, heals you, prepares you, and calls you into His destiny for your life, you must cling to Him as though you really are bound with a physical cord. The enemy will oppose you, but you are victorious over him through the powerful blood of Jesus.

CONFRONT

1. What does the shed blood of Jesus mean in your life? _____

   _____

   _____

   _____

   _____

2. How will you practically begin to "bind" yourself to Christ Jesus?

   _____

   _____

   _____

   _____

3. Do you need victory over the enemy in any area of your life? Ask God to enable you to walk in a deeper understanding of the blood. Apply the power of the blood and declare that the enemy must take his hands off you because of the blood! _____

   _____

   _____

   _____

   _____

CONQUER

What do the Scriptures below mean to you personally and how can you apply them in your life?

Ephesians 1:7 _____

_____

_____

_____

Colossians 1:13, 14 _____

_____

_____

_____

Colossians 2:13, 14 _____

_____

_____

_____

DAY 5: STAY IN THE HOUSE

Rahab received another instruction from the spies: Stay in the house (Josh. 2:19).

I say to you today: stay in the house. Stay in the covenant of God. Stay steadfast in your faith. Stay in the place of your God-given assignment. Stay under the spiritual covering God has provided for you.

You may not always understand why God hasn't worked yet on your behalf or brought your breakthrough. Don't allow your lack of understanding to cause you to walk out from under the umbrella of God's protection. Don't allow yourself to become discouraged or dismayed, because I assure you that God did not bring you out of bondage to watch you go back into bondage. He is ordering your footsteps. He is working all things together for your good.

If you want to be rescued, if you want God to move you into the future that will be marked by an abundance of life, if you want God to create for you a place in His history—then don't move away from God. Stay in the house!

As you go through the changes God is bringing to your life, remember that He is calling you into something far greater and more fulfilling than you have ever imagined. Be like Rahab: acknowledge that God is the Lord of the heavens and the earth; receive Jesus as your Savior and put yourself under the covering of His shed blood. And then, stay faithful in your relationship with Jesus. Don't be moved, but stay in the house!

CONFRONT

1. What does "stay in the house" mean to you? Be as specific as possible, writing about every area of your life you can think of. _____

_____

_____

_____

_____

2. Are you being tempted to "leave the house" in any way? What can you do to stay inside and cooperate with God's good plans for your life?

_____

_____

_____

_____

3. What is God asking you to change in your life? How can you stay in the house as you make these changes? _____

_____

_____

_____

_____

CONQUER

What do the Scriptures below mean to you personally and how can you apply them in your life?

Hebrews 6:12 _____

_____

_____

_____

Psalm 37:23 _____

_____

_____

_____

Romans 8:28 _____

_____

_____

_____

Lesson 4

DORCAS:
DEALING WITH OVERLOAD

To understand who Dorcas was and the challenges she faced, read Acts 9:36–42 and Chapter 4 of the book, *Deal With It!*

DAY 1: AUDIT YOUR LIFE

I believe the best way to avoid becoming overloaded and depleted, as Dorcas was, is to audit your life and make sure it is balanced. What do I mean by "audit your life"? In the financial world, an audit means balancing the deposits and withdrawals of money in an account. In life, if we have more withdrawals than deposits, we operate "in the red." Sooner or later, something is going to fall apart—health, an important endeavor, a highly-valued relationship or something else that really matters. Making too many withdrawals and not enough deposits will leave us feeling "bankrupt"—overloaded, discouraged, depleted, and exhausted.

A "life audit" is similar—it is taking a look at the deposits and withdrawals of our time, energy, creativity, commitment, and resources. A woman whose "life account" is depleted feels pressured and weary. When that happens, she loses her joy, her perspective, her sense of doing any one thing well, her gentleness, and her grace toward others. She becomes increasingly frustrated and overreacts to things she would normally take in stride.

The depleted woman's worst enemy often becomes her "inner-me." She sabotages her own work and relationships, and is more vulnerable to attacks from the enemy.

One of the enemy's favorite strategies is to wear you down. His best chance of defeating you is when you are "weary." He comes against people mentally, physically and spiritually. In order to resist and overcome his attacks, you must know your capacities, know your limits and do what is necessary in order to stay strong mentally, physically and spiritually.

CONFRONT

1. On a scale of 1–10, with 1 being "not at all" and 10 being "over the top," how weary and pressured do you feel? _____

   _____

   _____

   _____

   _____

2. How is the enemy attacking you mentally, physically, or spiritually right now? _____

   _____

   _____

   _____

   _____

3. On a separate piece of paper, begin to audit your life. Start by writing down the deposits and withdrawals in three areas: physically, mentally, and spiritually. Is there an imbalance? What changes can you begin to make to bring about better balance in these areas? _____

   _____

   _____

   _____

   _____

CONQUER

What do the Scriptures below mean to you personally and how can you apply them in your life?

Philippians 4:6 _____

_____

_____

_____

Luke 14:28 _____

_____

_____

_____

Hebrews 10:36 _____

_____

_____

_____

DAY 2: AUDIT YOUR STRENGTHS AND WEAKNESSES

To illustrate my point that we need to audit our strengths and weaknesses, I'd like to share a personal story with you:

In 1995, I traveled the world three times in just a few months, preaching the gospel and ministering to more than one million people that year. I was mentally and spiritually strong enough to do it, but I ended up in emergency rooms several times, so physically exhausted and dehydrated that I needed intravenous fluids to restore my body. On one occasion, an emergency room physician said to me, "You'll feel better after you've had a bag or two of this fluid." It took *seven* bags of fluids before my body said, "I've had enough." I was that dehydrated.

I am not as strong physically as I am mentally and spiritually. At the risk of almost oversimplifying my point, let's just say that my mental and spiritual capacities are my strengths, while my physical body is a weakness. Signs of pressure or weariness occur for me in my body before they do in my mind or in my spiritual life. Therefore, I must guard and protect myself physically because that is the weakest area of my life.

Likewise, you need to know your weaknesses. You can be assured that the enemy knows them, and that's where he will attack first and most often! Recognizing your weaknesses helps you to be more vigilant in guarding those areas of your life against weariness and against the enemy.

At the same time, you must also know your strengths, your dominant abilities and gifts, the things you naturally do well. The ministry God has given you will draw on your God-given strengths. But, those same strengths are the areas in which you are likely to become overextended and exhausted. Often the enemy attempts to wear you out when you are doing the right things!

Audit your strengths and your weaknesses. Work on your weaknesses, but not to the point that you become depleted. At the same time, do not allow your strengths to become weaknesses because you exercise them to the point of exhaustion.

CONFRONT

1. What are your greatest strengths? _____

   _____

   _____

   _____

   _____

   _____

   _____

2. What are your greatest weaknesses? _____

   _____

   _____

   _____

   _____

   _____

   _____

3. How can you make sure that you do not exercise your strengths to the point of exhaustion and that you grow stronger in your areas of weakness? _____

_____

_____

_____

_____

CONQUER

What do the Scriptures below mean to you personally and how can you apply them in your life?

Galatians 6:9 _____

_____

_____

_____

2 Corinthians 12:9 _____

_____

_____

_____

Ephesians 6:10 _____

_____

_____

_____

DAY 3: AUDIT YOUR MOTIVES AND PRIORITIES

First Samuel 16:7 says that "the LORD looks at the heart" (NKJV). That tells me that our motives are extremely important to Him. A motive is the "why" behind "what" we do. If you are overloaded, out of balance, and depleted, you need to understand why. Ask yourself why you push yourself so hard. Why do you go beyond your limitations? What are you trying to prove? To whom? Are you doing something that seems good, but isn't what God is calling you to do at the moment? Then it's time to audit your motives.

Once you have determined why you do what you do, you can begin to set priorities. Anything you do from wrong motives (selfishness, fear, jealousy, insecurity, pride, or for any other ungodly reason) may need to move down on your priority list!

I believe our priorities should reflect the Lord's assignments for our lives. Above all, we are all assigned to know Him, to love Him, and to follow Him. After that, our assignments differ. My foremost assignments from the Lord are my husband, my children, and my ministry. Therefore, I prioritize my husband, my children, and my ministry. When other things clamor for my time and attention, they threaten my ability to fully commit to and engage in my assignments.

If you are going to live a victorious life, you cannot allow things that are low on your priority list to become confused with your greater priorities. You really cannot afford to allow those lesser things to detract from your greater purpose or to water down the effort you put into your God-assigned relationships, visions, and tasks.

There's only so much energy you can expend, so much time you can allot, and so much of yourself you can give. I urge you to operate out of pure, godly motives and to set your priorities accordingly. Yes, there will be some things that don't get done and some people who may be disappointed. But at the end of every day, it is God you must please, not people. And it is His assignments, not anyone else's, you must put first.

CONFRONT

1. What motivates you to do the things you do? How can you replace ungodly motives with godly motives? _____

   _____

   _____

   _____

   _____

2. What are your priorities? _____

_____

_____

_____

_____

3. Look at your list of priorities in question 2. Beginning with your first priority, how far down the list can you reasonably go before you become pressured and weary? _____

_____

_____

_____

_____

CONQUER

What do the Scriptures below mean to you personally and how can you apply them in your life?

Psalm 139:23 _____

_____

_____

_____

Matthew 6:33 _____

_____

_____

_____

Colossians 3:14–17 _____

_____

_____

_____

DAY 4: AUDIT YOUR MINISTRY TO YOURSELF AND TO OTHERS

True ministry to others begins with ministry to the self. I'm not talking about a "me-first" attitude, but the truth is, you can't lead a person to Christ unless you know Him; you can't preach the Word of God effectively unless you have read and studied it; you can't feed others if you don't have any food; you can't love others unless you first love yourself; you can't give away what you don't have—and that includes time, energy, and creativity as well as money and material resources. It is important that you see yourself as God sees you, because what you believe about yourself and the way you treat yourself determines what you believe about others and how you treat them.

When ministering to others, realize that you can't be all things to all people. There are only so many people you can genuinely help at any given time. Also, trying to be "God" to others is a sure formula for burnout. Be cautious if people always seem to be turning to you to solve their problems and meet their needs. God wants you to help others, but never to take sole responsibility for their lives. Only He belongs in that position of responsibility and authority.

Whatever situation you find yourself in as you minister to others and to yourself, pray for wisdom and strategy, do the best you can, and let God be God in every way.

CONFRONT

1. What needs to change about your ministry to yourself?

_____

_____

_____

_____

_____

_____

2. What needs to change about your ministry to others? _____

_____

_____

_____

_____

3. Are there any relationships or situations that you need to give over
   to the Lord? _____

_____

_____

_____

_____

CONQUER

What do the Scriptures below mean to you personally and how can you
apply them in your life?

Matthew 22:39 _____

_____

_____

_____

Romans 14:12 _____

_____

_____

_____

1 Peter 5:7 _____

_____

_____

_____

DAY 5: MANAGE YOUR LIFE

It isn't enough simply to audit your life and its various components. You must also take responsibility for your own life and begin to manage it according to God's principles. You must manage your time, your energy, and your creativity—and devote those resources to the things that most closely align with what God has called you to do.

Managing your life demands that you:

> Learn to say, "No" and "Enough."
> Raise up people to help you.
> Learn to live a balanced life.
> Replenish what has been depleted.
> Allow your spirit to be restored.
> Find what works.

Why is it important to audit and manage your life? So you can move toward God's destiny without stress! I believe strongly that God has an appointed time for your blessing, your breakthrough, and your healing. But if you arrive at that appointed moment, and are too weary or too paralyzed to give birth, you can miss out on what God desires for you to have.

When Peter spoke to Dorcas' body, he said one word: *"Arise!"* God speaks that word to you today. To arise is to "stand up and bring forward, to come into your being"—to become powerful, to walk into the wholeness God has for you.

If you are wearied and pressured, God says to you, "Arise!"

If you have poured yourself out for others to the point of exhaustion, God says to you, "Arise!"

If your sense of destiny has been lost amid the stresses of everyday life, God says to you, "Arise!"

Put death on hold. Turn to God and ask Him to restore your soul!

If you are feeling today that everybody is pulling at you, wanting a bigger and bigger piece of you, deal with it by asking Jesus to give you the courage to say "No" and "Enough!" and to take on only those things that He asks you to do. Now is the time to be strengthened and renewed so you can move forward into the fullness of what God still has for you to birth in your future!

CONFRONT

1. Practically and personally, what needs to happen in order for you to manage your life? _____

_____

_____

_____

_____

_____

2. In what areas of your life do you need to hear and respond to God's call to arise? _____

_____

_____

_____

_____

_____

3. What steps can you take in order to be replenished, so that you can arise and move into everything God has for you? _____

_____

_____

_____

_____

CONQUER

What do the Scriptures below mean to you personally and how can you apply them in your life?

Ecclesiastes 3:1 _____

_____

_____

_____

Hebrews 6:10 _____

_____

_____

_____

Matthew 11:28 _____

_____

_____

_____

Lesson 5

GOMER:
DEALING WITH YOUR PAIN

To understand who Gomer was and the challenges she faced, read Hosea 1:2, 3; 2:4, 5; and 3:1–3, and Chapter 5 of the book, *Deal With It!*

DAY 1: THE EFFECTS OF TRAUMA

A woman who has been traumatized often feels sorrow, sadness, depression, despair, and a sense of loss. Her heart is broken and she suffers from deep, internal wounds.

Often, a woman who has been traumatized can't think clearly—she sometimes feels confused and scattered in her thinking to the point where she may feel as if she is going crazy. She sometimes can't remember things she once knew well. She sometimes can't put two thoughts together in a logical way.

Trauma also throws off a person's sense of emotional balance. Most people know how to balance the everyday stresses and strains of life, but a person who has been wounded often has a very hard time achieving and maintaining emotional equilibrium. Simple things—such as everyday experiences, decisions, and problems that other people find routine—often become difficult.

Finally, when a person has been deeply hurt or emotionally bruised, her self-esteem always takes a hit. A woman who is traumatized feels "depersonalized"—less of a person. Her self-identity and her self-worth are stripped away; she feels vulnerable; and she loses her sense of individuality, of what makes her unique. There's a feeling that her life has been irreversibly tarnished and diminished.

God's Word tells us that Jesus feels your sorrows and declares that Jesus is your High Priest, who has a supernatural ability to sympathize with your weaknesses (see Heb. 4:15). Jesus feels what you feel. Jesus knows how you hurt. Jesus is capable of empathizing completely with your condition and your past wounding. Jesus not only knows that you have been hurt, but He knows that you have *felt* hurt. He understands fully the wounding of your soul.

The truth of God's Word to you is this: God wants to heal *your* hurting heart! God wants to restore your fractured mind; God wants you to have emotional balance; and God wants to raise your self-esteem. He is for you, and He wants you whole in every way.

CONFRONT

   1. What traumas or emotional hurts have you endured? _____

     _____

     _____

     _____

     _____

   2. How has your trauma affected you? _____

     _____

     _____

     _____

     _____

   3. Do you now have hope that Jesus wants to heal you and make you whole? _____

     _____

     _____

     _____

     _____

CONQUER

What do the Scriptures below mean to you personally and how can you apply them in your life?

Luke 4:18, 19 _____

_____

_____

_____

Romans 12:2 _____

_____

_____

_____

3 John 2 _____

_____

_____

_____

DAY 2: BE SLOW TO JUDGE

If I had chosen to pass judgment on all the people God has put in my life, I would have missed out on some incredible blessings, because most of the people God has sent my way have been like David's band of "misfits." They didn't "have it all together;" they didn't look or act right. But God said to me, "I will raise them up to be a mighty armor for you, to possess My promise to you. I have placed them in your path."

I don't know what led Gomer to do what she did. Only God knows how far Gomer had come. I do know, however, that we are not to play the part of God and be anyone's judge! Judgment belongs in the hands of God who is the only One who knows the heart of a person, " . . . for the LORD does not see as man sees; for man looks at the outward appearance, but the LORD looks at the heart" (1 Sam. 16:7, NKJV).

Don't ever think you are immune from doing certain things. If you become desperate enough, you just may! You may find yourself with deep unmet needs—and at that point, you are likely to take desperate action. Don't ever think you would be above sleeping in a defiled bed if you were desperate to feed your starving children. Don't ever think you wouldn't enter a wrong relationship if you were desperate to feel love and to hear kind words. Don't think you would be above doing some crazy thing if you were desperate for attention or affection.

Even if you have not done something desperate, you may have thought about it! Don't think you're exempt from anything! "The heart is deceitful above all things, and desperately wicked; who can know it?" (Jer. 17:9). Don't think you are above or beyond sin, and do not judge others. Only God is a just Judge, and we are to leave people in God's hands.

CONFRONT

1. Have you ever missed out on a blessing in your life because of judgment? _____

   _____

   _____

   _____

2. Are you guilty of judging anyone right now? If so, pray and ask God to forgive you and to help you refrain from judging people in the future.

   _____

   _____

   _____

   _____

3. In your own words why is it so dangerous to judge people? _____

   _____

   _____

   _____

CONQUER

What do the Scriptures below mean to you personally and how can you apply them in your life?

Matthew 7:1, 2 _____

_____

_____

_____

Romans 2:1 _____

_____

_____

_____

Romans 14:3 _____

_____

_____

_____

DAY 3: GRIEVE BEFORE YOU GO

Trauma requires healing, and healing requires grieving. Expressing pain is part of the grieving process. Grieving is vital to closure and it is part of the healing process anytime you have lost something precious. I encourage you to move through all the stages of grief explained below so that you can truly deal with your losses and be prepared to move into everything God has for you.

- *Denial.* First, there's denial—"I can't believe this has happened." In denial, you may be tempted to say that your loss did not affect you, even when everyone knows it did. You cannot begin to heal until you turn from denial and acknowledge your pain.

- *Anger.* Second, you may become angry for being hurt or rejected and say things like, "I didn't deserve this!"

- *Bargaining.* Third, there's the bargaining stage—"If this happens . . . then . . . If God will . . . then I'll . . ." Because God doesn't want you to stay stuck in the past, He doesn't bargain with you; He begins to heal you.

- *Depression.* Fourth, there's depression, which leaves you in despair and overwhelming sadness. When you are depressed you have no hope—and hope is what gives you the power to go on.

- *Acceptance.* Finally, there's acceptance that what has happened, has happened. The truth is that some things may never be made "right" in your life, but you must accept them. Acceptance involves burying what is dead. It's leaving what is "over." It's not only accepting that the past was the past, but also accepting that your future is still ahead of you.

Don't try to get to "acceptance" without going through the other stages. Only if you will go through *all* the stages will you be able to stand at the end of the process and say, "This happened. It hurt and I was angry about it. I no longer am trying to 'deal' with God about it. I've been depressed about it but I am no longer depressed. I accept this as a part of my history, but it is *not* a part of my future."

CONFRONT

1. Have you thoroughly grieved all of your losses? If not, ask God to help you. _____

   _____

   _____

   _____

2. Have you accepted the pain of your past? If not, ask God to help you.

   _____

   _____

   _____

   _____

3. Can you say with confidence that the painful things that have happened to you in the past will not affect your future? If not, ask God to help you get to that point. _____

_____

_____

_____

_____

CONQUER

What do the Scriptures below mean to you personally and how can you apply them in your life?

Ecclesiastes 3:4 _____

_____

_____

_____

Psalm 30:5b _____

_____

_____

_____

Psalm 126:6 _____

_____

_____

_____

DAY 4: HEALING IS A PROCESS

Trauma changes us. Healing also changes us. In fact, God turns trauma around for our good. What once was so exceedingly painful and horrible can become, by God's power, a driving force that produces very positive results! The Bible says, "All things work together for good to those who love God . . ." (Rom.

8:28, NKJV). God's ultimate plan for you is *always* good. He has an appointed time for healing everything negative that you have been through in your past. It doesn't matter what happened, when it happened, or where it happened, He is here to heal you *now.*

Wounding was an *event;* healing is a *process.* And *forgiveness* is the first step in your healing process. Ask God to forgive you of your sins, including the things you have done to yourself. Also ask God to heal you of what you could not prevent and never deserved. Ask Him to give you the grace to forgive those who have sinned against you and allow the love and acceptance of Jesus to heal your broken heart and make you whole.

The second step in healing is to choose to *receive* God's forgiveness in your life and move forward. Do not let guilt hold you back from everything God has for you. He forgives you completely and you need to forgive yourself as thoroughly as He does.

Third, as you heal, you will need to bury what is dead. Leave what is "over." Get on with what God has for you! When God's answer is "no," you must decide to say "yes" to the future He holds out to you.

Fourth, in the process of healing, you must *get up and go on.* Who knows what good things God has for you in your future? Who knows the abundance of life He has designed for you? You *won't* know unless you rise up and walk toward your future!

CONFRONT

1. In what ways do you need to forgive yourself? _____

   _____

   _____

   _____

2. In what ways do you need to forgive other people? _____

   _____

   _____

   _____

3. What do you need to bury in order to get up and walk toward your future? _____

_____

_____

_____

_____

CONQUER

What do the Scriptures below mean to you personally and how can you apply them in your life?

Psalm 86:5 _____

_____

_____

_____

2 Corinthians 12:9 _____

_____

_____

_____

Joshua 1:9 _____

_____

_____

_____

DAY 5: LET GOD DEFINE YOU

People called Gomer a "harlot." They labeled her according to her profession. And because they saw her profession as being shameful, they saw Gomer as being shameful.

But how did *God* see Gomer? What name did *God* have for her?

Gomer's name means "beloved." God saw Gomer as His "beloved"!

Let me share briefly some of the names God calls you:

God calls you "Beloved." One of the greatest challenges in life is to accept the unconditional love of God. One way to receive His love after you have been wounded by trauma is to say, "I will not base my actions on *feelings.* I will base my actions on what God's Word says." You must also face your fears, including your fear of love. Receiving love requires a degree of vulnerability, and vulnerability is very difficult for a wounded person. It's hard to face fears, but you *must* do so if you are to overcome them.

You must begin to praise God for the truth that He has already accepted you. In fact, His unconditional love is chasing you down. God loves you. He is pursuing you.

God calls you "Redeemed." Jesus has redeemed you. To redeem is to regain possession by repurchase, to rescue or deliver, to pay a ransom to free a person from bondage. That's what Jesus did for you on the Cross. You *are* delivered. You *are* free. You *are* rescued from your sin. The past is past. It's over. You are redeemed.

God calls you "Useful." He has something for you to birth! God redeemed you so you can fulfill His assignment on your life. He has a mission for you to accomplish and He has designed you *perfectly* for the assignment on your life.

It's okay to hurt. But you must heal and move forward. If your past pain is hindering you in any way, deal with it by allowing Jesus to heal you everywhere you hurt. Don't let your history hinder you from your destiny!

CONFRONT

1. How can you practically open your heart to better receive God's unconditional love? _____

_____

_____

_____

2. What specifically will you say to God in order to praise Him for accepting you? _____

_____

_____

_____

3. In your own words, what does it mean that you are redeemed?

_____

_____

_____

_____

CONQUER

What do the Scriptures below mean to you personally and how can you apply them in your life?

Ephesians 1:7 _____

_____

_____

_____

Jeremiah 1:5 _____

_____

_____

_____

Isaiah 43:1 _____

_____

_____

_____

Lesson 6

HANNAH:
Dealing with Resentment

To understand who Hannah was and the challenges she faced, read 1 Samuel 1:1–20 and Chapter 6 of the book, *Deal With It!*

DAY 1: DIVISION IS A DEVICE OF THE ENEMY

Paul told the Corinthians that we are not to be ignorant of the devil's devices (see 2 Cor. 2:11) and one of his devices is to create division. In fact, "divide and conquer" is one of his favorite strategies. He wants to confuse you so that you will have a divided mind and he wants to break your heart into a million pieces so that you will never get your life together again. The enemy knows that with a divided mind and broken heart, you will question your faith and fail to reach your destiny.

The devil comes to divide you and break you personally, but he also comes to divide and break up your family, your church, and your friendships. We know we are broken and divided when we can't get along with people, when we don't think they do anything right, when their presence gets on our nerves, or when we speak sharply to them for no apparent reason. This kind of division indicates a lack of unity, and where there is no unity, there is strife.

In order to overcome division, we must walk in unity. But unity isn't easy. It takes effort, diligence, and labor. That's what the word *endeavoring* means in Ephesians 4:3, which says: "endeavoring to keep the unity of the Spirit in the bond of peace" (NKJV). What is the work we are to do? It's the work of staying in the Word, meditating on it day and night. It's the work of staying in Christ, trusting Him, and looking to Him daily to do His work. It's the work of walking daily in the Spirit.

God is love, and if we are filled with His Spirit, love will be our automatic response in every situation (see 1 John 4:13–15.) If we are walking in the Spirit on a daily basis, love will flow from us—and that's what it takes to defeat division.

CONFRONT

1. Has the devil sown division in any of your relationships? How can you express love and make the situation right? _____

   _____

   _____

   _____

   _____

   _____

   _____

2. How's your love walk? What can you do to more intentionally love people? _____

   _____

   _____

   _____

   _____

   _____

   _____

3. In your own words, why is love the key to overcoming division?

   _____

   _____

   _____

   _____

CONQUER

What do the Scriptures below mean to you personally and how can you apply them in your life?

1 Peter 4:8 _____

_____

_____

_____

James 3:16 _____

_____

_____

_____

John 17:11 _____

_____

_____

_____

DAY 2: THE ROOT OF JEALOUSY

Female rivalry is nearly always rooted in jealousy, and virtually every woman is jealous of another woman at some point. Female jealousy is rooted in fear—specifically the fear that she can be replaced. When a woman is no longer afraid she can be replaced, she is no longer jealous.

In order to break free from such fear, a woman must first be set free spiritually, which means she must know who she is in Christ. She must come to know and believe in her spirit that she will *never* be replaced because God loves her specifically and has a purpose for her on this earth. She must understand her position in Christ—that it is secure, and that she has been created as one-of-a-kind. When that happens, fear and jealousy fade away.

To defeat fear in your life, first identify what you *think* is the truth of your situation and then see if it lines up with the truth of God's Word. Face up to what you are believing about yourself, your future, and your relationship with God—and then see if your beliefs agree with God's Word.

1 John 4:18 says, "There is no fear in love; but perfect love casts out fear . . ." (NKJV). Why? Because love is total security. When you know that God loves you with an infinite, unconditional, and unchanging love, then your security is unshakable; your confidence is rock solid; and your self-esteem cannot be threatened because it is based on the way God values and esteems you.

If you are jealous or fearful, then check your "love status." What do you not believe about God's love for you? What hidden motives, desires, or attitudes are keeping you from experiencing God's love?

He loves you—more than you can imagine. He wants you to know His affection in a deeply personal way, stay confident in His care for you, and be at peace in His love. Then there won't be any room in your heart for jealousy or fear.

CONFRONT

1. Do you struggle with jealousy? How can you begin to love the person(s) you are jealous of? _____

   _____

   _____

   _____

   _____

2. What beliefs do you have that are contrary to God's Word? What Scriptures can you use to bring truth to those areas of your thinking?

   _____

   _____

   _____

   _____

   _____

3. What are some of the things God thinks and says about you in His Word? (Use Scriptures you already know, or use a concordance to help you find them.) _____

_____

_____

_____

_____

CONQUER

What do the Scriptures below mean to you personally and how can you apply them in your life?

Proverbs 14:30 _____

_____

_____

_____

Psalm 34:4 _____

_____

_____

_____

Isaiah 35:4 _____

_____

_____

_____

DAY 3: LEAVE IT WITH THE LORD

No person can heal what is broken inside you. No human being can restore your hope. No spouse can make it right. No child can solve the problem. Only God can give you a deep awareness of how infinitely valuable and precious you are to Him, and what a great destiny He has for you. Only God can see and meet the unmet needs in your life that even you don't recognize. Only God can fix your heart. Only God can mend your mind.

Only God can do what needs to be done, so don't demand from any person what only God can give. God's Word doesn't say to cast all your cares on your pastor, a committee, your social club, your boss, or your best friend. There are cares only God can handle; there are bondages only God can break; there are situations only God can resolve; there are circumstances only God can change.

Let me encourage you to be like Hannah, who allowed her desperation to have a child drive her to the only One who had the answer to her dilemma—the Lord. And when you are that desperate for a touch from God, the opinions of people won't deter you. When you are sick and tired of being sick and tired, you'll do whatever it takes to get your answer from God.

Some people today aren't desperate enough. They are content to live with their pain. But God has more for you, so stir yourself up today and press toward Him. Take your problem to Him and leave it there!

CONFRONT

1. Do you have a need that is deep enough to drive you to push through any resistance to get to God? _____

   _____

   _____

   _____

   _____

2. What is it that only God can handle in your life? _____

   _____

   _____

   _____

   _____

3. What does it mean to leave your problem with the Lord? Practically, how will you do that? _____

_____

_____

_____

_____

CONQUER

What do the Scriptures below mean to you personally and how can you apply them in your life?

Psalm 6:9 _____

_____

_____

Psalm 50:15 _____

_____

_____

_____

John 14:1 _____

_____

_____

_____

DAY 4: PERSEVERE AND TRUST

It's not enough for you to pour your heart out to God; you must persevere in pouring out your heart to Him until you get His answer back.

That answer may come as you read God's Word, as you hear a sermon on television, in church, or at a conference, or it may come from His still, small voice speaking in your heart. The answer may come into your mind and heart in a flash, or it may come to you slowly over time. But when you cry out to God from the depths of your heart, He *will* answer you. And, He'll answer you in a way that will make you *know* it is His answer. What He says will happen, *will* happen.

Hannah's prayer of desperation was a prayer of faith. She looked to God to do for her what no person could do. She trusted God to hear and answer her, even if everybody around her misunderstood her. She trusted Him and had faith in Him.

God's Word says that faith has the power to give "life to the dead and calls those things which do not exist as though they did" (Rom. 4:17, NKJV). Faith causes you to walk in the spirit realm and to put your belief in what God can do, is doing, and will do—rather than on what you see around you. The only way to have that kind of faith is to rest in God and trust in God no matter what.

Faith that perseveres and rests in God says to Him:

"I trust You to give me a baby, even if I'm ninety years old."

"I trust You to provide for me, even if my cupboard is bare."

"I trust You to heal me, even if the doctor says I have no hope."

"I trust You to save my children, even though they say they want nothing to do with You."

"I trust You. I trust You. I trust You!"

CONFRONT

1. What is faith and why does it make a difference in your life?

_____

_____

_____

_____

2. What are you trusting God for today? _____

_____

_____

_____

3. Briefly write about some of God's answers to your prayers in the past. That will help build your faith to persevere in the present. _____

_____

_____

_____

_____

CONQUER

What do the Scriptures below mean to you personally and how can you apply them in your life?

Psalm 9:10 _____

_____

_____

_____

Psalm 145:18 _____

_____

_____

_____

Jeremiah 33:3 _____

_____

_____

_____

DAY 5: BE WILLING TO WORK

There is a time to pour out your heart before the Lord with anguish and grief—and there is also a time to get up, wipe your tears, and walk away saying, "I believe it is so," even before there's any visible evidence.

Hannah took action and began to walk in faith. After she had prayed, she wiped her tears, put a smile on her face, and said to herself, *God is at work. I don't know how. I don't know when. I don't know all the details, but God is at work.* That's what it means to trust—to move into position to receive the very thing God has promised.

Nothing about Hannah's situation had changed, but everything about Hannah had changed. She had determined within herself that she would do what she could do, so that God could do what He could do!

I don't know what you're trusting God for today, but you have a part to play in it. You have to put feet to your faith and walk out what you're believing God to do!

If you are believing God for a business, start working! Get a business plan. Find property. Start advertising. Get a loan if necessary. Learn how to make the business work.

If you are believing God for a ministry, start working! Be diligent to study the Word and preach to the shower tiles if you have to. Vacuum the sanctuary or serve as an usher. Teach the two-year-olds.

When you start walking in total assurance that God has heard you and will answer you, and when you start putting action and works to your faith, your dream will begin to be established in you. It will grow in you until God's appointed time for it to be delivered into this world, where it can lead to the expansion of God's great kingdom. Whatever you are believing God to do— start working at it!

CONFRONT

1. How can you trust God in a very specific situation in your life right now? _____

_____

_____

_____

_____

2. What are you believing God for? _____

_____

_____

_____

_____

3. What actions can you take today to demonstrate your faith in God?

_____

_____

_____

_____

CONQUER

What do the Scriptures below mean to you personally and how can you apply them in your life?

James 2:17 _____

_____

_____

_____

Proverbs 3:5, 6 _____

_____

_____

_____

Psalm 37:3, 4 _____

_____

_____

_____

Lesson 7

MARY MAGDALENE:
Dealing with Sin

To understand who Mary Magdalene was and the challenges she faced, read Luke 8:2; John 20:1–3, 11–14; and Chapter 7 of the book, *Deal With It!*

DAY 1: BE MADE NEW

Mary Magdalene was a woman with a tormented past. Depravity, despair, and loneliness must have plagued her before Jesus changed her. As He changed her, He can change you—no matter who you are or what you have done: God's Word says: "Therefore, if anyone is in Christ, he is a new creation; old things have passed away; behold, all things have become new. Now all things are of God, who has reconciled us to Himself through Jesus Christ, and has given us the ministry of reconciliation, that is, that God was in Christ reconciling the world to Himself, not imputing their trespasses to them, and has committed to us the word of reconciliation. Now then, we are ambassadors for Christ" (2 Cor. 5:17–20, NKJV).

The Greek word for *in* when referring to being "in Christ" denotes position—a relationship of rest. The only way you can ever overcome your condition is by knowing your position. Knowing "church" doesn't change you. Knowing a little bit of Hebrew and Greek doesn't change you. Even knowing Bible verses doesn't change you if they are only in your head and not in your heart. Only knowing Christ and your position in Him changes you! When you know who He is, then you can know who you are in Him.

You are not of this world; you are *in Christ*.

To be a "new creation" in Christ means to be recently made, unused, fresh, and unprecedented. The old has passed away. There is a new way for you to look, to think, to talk, to walk, to act, to respond to life.

God does not determine your future by the past experiences of your life. He sees the "end" of you—He sees down the line into your future and sees you transformed. He sees good things developing in you and good things coming to you and good things happening through you. God never binds you to your past—He frees you for your future.

God looks at you and calls you by what you *will* be. He calls you "anointed prophet," "saint," "highly favored," "great soul winner," "world evangelist," "terrific mom," "best teacher" or "awesome friend." Don't be so conditioned by looking at your situation that you forget God is way ahead of you and is taking you to where you *will* be.

CONFRONT

1. For you personally, what does it mean to be "a new creation"?

   _____

   _____

   _____

   _____

2. List some of your past sins and struggles. Then, go back and draw a line through them and write their opposites. That's how God sees you!

   _____

   _____

   _____

   _____

3. As a new creation, how will you respond differently to the things that once tempted or hindered you? _____

   _____

   _____

   _____

CONQUER

What do the Scriptures below mean to you personally and how can you apply them in your life?

2 Corinthians 5:17 _____

_____

_____

_____

Ephesians 1:7 _____

_____

_____

_____

Colossians 2:10 _____

_____

_____

_____

DAY 2: "A" STANDS FOR ACTIVATOR

Mary was a woman who had been labeled by life. Has a label been put on your life, such as *poor, abused, dumb, unattractive,* or *sick?*

Years ago I learned the ABC's for confronting life's labels: "A" stands for activator; "B" stands for belief, and "C" stands for consequences. In the rest of the chapter, I will explain what will happen when you apply these ABC principles to your life. I believe doing this will help you become free from the unfair labels that have been placed upon you.

"A" *stands for "activator."* Identify the experience, conversation, or situation that "activated" or started the label-making process in your life. You didn't just wake up one day with the belief that you cannot stand yourself. You have probably had that opinion for some time through a number of defining moments, many of which were from your childhood. It's important to ask yourself, *When was this negative label first attached to my life, and by whom?*

Psalm 139:14 says that you are "fearfully and wonderfully made." The word *fearfully* means "reverently." To be *wonderfully* made means "to be distinctively and uniquely" created.

Many women today don't value themselves because they are living by comparison. They are looking to people around them or to models in magazines to tell them what they *should* be, and by comparison, pointing out to them what they *aren't*. The truth of God is that you are a designer original! You are not a cheap imitation or a copy. Embrace your distinctiveness! That's where you'll find your value.

Very often what other people see as your faults or foibles are the very things that God sees as your best assets waiting to be redeemed, strengthened, and fashioned in such a way that they bring glory to Him.

What you are criticizing about yourself and what others seem to "hate" about you may very well be the things that God is seeking to use for His purposes. God knew what He was doing when He created you!

Choose only the labels that God puts on your life. Activate *only* what He says.

CONFRONT

1. What labels have people tried to attach to you? How can you "unstitch" the labels that have been put on your life? _____

   _____

   _____

   _____

2. What Scriptures can you use to get God's Word about you established in your heart? _____

   _____

   _____

   _____

3. What is your most unique quality? How might God use that?

_____

_____

_____

_____

CONQUER

What do the Scriptures below mean to you personally and how can you apply them in your life?

John 17:17 _____

_____

_____

_____

Psalm 119:105 _____

_____

_____

_____

Colossians 3:16a _____

_____

_____

_____

DAY 3: "B" STANDS FOR BELIEF

What label do you believe with such intensity that it has become your dominant thought?

Behavioral scientists tell us that a negative thought attached with a feeling can be repeated in a person's mind as many as six hundred times a day! It becomes what is called a *dominant thought*. Dominant thoughts drive behavior and end up controlling a person's life.

Are your dominant thoughts coming from God's Word or from someone's opinion?

When you know who you are, you develop a very solid self-esteem. You *believe* in yourself because you believe in what God says you are, what you are capable of doing, and can have.

Part of coming to that belief is recognizing that the Word of God applies directly to *you*.

It's reading Romans 8:28 and saying, "All things are working together for *my* good because I am loved by God and called according to His purpose."

It's reading Psalm 35:27 and saying, "God's desire for *me* is that I prosper in all things. He takes pleasure in my prosperity."

Let me remind you of two things the enemy will tell you anytime you have a dominant thought that isn't based on God's Word:

- *You are the only one in the world with this problem.* The enemy tries to isolate us from others. And when we buy into that lie, we *feel* isolated and lonely. Isolation and loneliness always are accompanied by frustration because we are creatures who were made for fellowship, love, and relationship—not isolation.

God's truth is that you are not alone. God is with you 24/7. He never leaves you nor forsakes you.

- *You will* always *have this problem.* The enemy will tell us that our situation cannot be resolved, settled, changed, or cured. When we buy into that lie, we feel despair. Hope and joy are drained out of us. And when that happens, depression fills that void.

God's truth is that *all* things are possible with God. Absolutely *nothing* is impossible.

CONFRONT

1. How have you reacted emotionally and behaviorally since a label became stuck on you? _____

_____

_____

_____

_____

_____

2. What behaviors and habits have resulted from your dominant thoughts and beliefs? _____

_____

_____

_____

_____

_____

3. How will you replace dominant thoughts that are not based on God's Word with new ones that are? _____

_____

_____

_____

_____

_____

CONQUER

What do the Scriptures below mean to you personally and how can you apply them in your life?

Isaiah 41:10 _____

_____

_____

_____

Joshua 1:9 _____

_____

_____

_____

Matthew 19:26 _____

_____

_____

_____

DAY 4: "C" STANDS FOR CONSEQUENCES

Typically, when your mind is renewed, your beliefs change, and then your behaviors change. Occasionally, though, the opposite is true and renewal begins first in behavior. When a person begins to adopt new behaviors and habits based on God's Word, the new habits create a new character, and a new character creates a new destiny. Habits can drive beliefs.

Either way, it's ultimately up to you to *choose* to change your behavior, and that includes changing the atmosphere and the associations of your life.

That was certainly the case with Mary Magdalene. She refused to reinforce the labels life had placed on her by remaining in the environment and in the relationships that first attached those labels to her. She changed her atmosphere and her associations.

This woman with such a tainted past was so transformed that she became friends with Salome and Mary, the mother of James and Joses (Mark 15:40). She began hanging out with Mary, the mother of Jesus (John 19:25). She became close to Joanna, the wife of Chuza, who was King Herod's steward (Luke 8:2, 3 and 24:10). She became a woman of influence, associating with influential women.

Mary Magdalene went from night to day. She went from walking the streets to walking with Jesus. She went from bondage to freedom. She went from oppression and depression to joy and fulfillment. She went from being filled with evil to being filled with peace, prosperity, and love.

Mary Magdalene was not only *changed* from her past, but she was given the hope and promise for the future. She was transformed for her future.

CONFRONT

1. What do you need to change about your atmosphere or environment in order to leave your labels behind and enjoy the new life God has for you? _____

   _____

   _____

   _____

   _____

2. Which associations or relationships do you need to walk away from in order to leave your labels behind and enjoy the new life God has for you? _____

   _____

   _____

   _____

   _____

3. What kind of new environment do you need in order to reach your potential in God and how will you begin to develop it? What new associations do you need and how will you begin to develop them?

   _____

   _____

   _____

   _____

CONQUER

What do the Scriptures below mean to you personally and how can you apply them in your life?

Isaiah 43:18, 19 _____

_____

_____

_____

Romans 8:1, 2 _____

_____

_____

_____

Romans 6:6 _____

_____

_____

_____

DAY 5: HOLD ON TO YOUR PROMISE

When Mary Magdalene first saw Jesus' empty tomb, she said, "I do not know where they have laid Him" (John 20:13, NKJV). The Bible says then she turned around and saw Jesus standing there, but she did not recognize Him. She could not believe that He was alive. Her promise, her dream, her hope was standing right in front of her, but she could not perceive it, she could not "see" with her faith, and she could not "believe" it was so.

Mary Magdalene couldn't get her eyes off the problem—the empty tomb, the not knowing where Jesus was. And because she couldn't get her eyes off the problem, she couldn't see the Problem Solver. Because she couldn't get her eyes off what had died, she couldn't see the power of the resurrected Christ standing right in front of her.

Open your spiritual eyes! See that God is working on your behalf. See that God is causing your seed to grow and that a harvest is coming. See that God is preparing you for the destiny that is still to come.

I don't know what dream you had from God. But I do know this: He never intended for it to die forever. He intends for that dream to live and produce a harvest that will extend on until eternity. He intends for that dream and that destiny to be fulfilled in you.

What is your dream?

What is it that you once were so passionate about?

What is it that you once fasted and prayed for?

What precisely has "died" on the inside of you?

Today is the day to regain your focus and deal with what has died in your life. Get your eyes on the future God has for you.

Today is the day to start to replace all of life's lies and labels with God's truth.

Today is the day to speak the Word, meditate on the Word, and act on the Word.

Today is the day to look again at the talents and gifts God has placed in you. Today is the day for that dream to be resurrected!

Today is the day to rise up and begin to birth the dream that God put in your heart.

Stop weeping and see the Resurrection standing before you! Put your trust in Him and reclaim the promise He placed in your heart.

CONFRONT

1. Has something important to you died—a dream, a desire, an aspiration? What is it? _____

   _____

   _____

   _____

   _____

2. Are you focusing on a dream you think has died or are you focusing on God's ability to revive it? _____

   _____

   _____

   _____

   _____

3. What adjustments can you make in your thinking and in your
   behavior as you stir up your faith and begin to focus on what God
   will do for you? _____

   _____

   _____

   _____

   _____

CONQUER

What do the Scriptures below mean to you personally and how can you
apply them in your life?

Romans 4:20, 21 _____

_____

_____

_____

Ephesians 3:20, 21 _____

_____

_____

_____

1 Thessalonians 5:24 _____

_____

_____

_____

Lesson 8

THE SHUNAMMITE WOMAN:
DEALING WITH YOUR RELATIONSHIPS

To understand who the Shunammite woman was and the challenges she faced, read 2 Kings 4:8–17 and Chapter 8 of the book, *Deal With It!*

DAY 1: FOLLOW A LEADER

The Shunammite woman chose wisely when she associated herself with Elijah. By God's grace, she recognized that Elijah had a vision for her life that was worth seeing, a word for her life that was worth hearing, a perception of her purpose in life that was worth pursuing, and a faith in his heart that was worth following.

None of us make it alone. We all follow somebody. We follow those who have gone before. We follow those who are more mature. We follow teachers and mentors and leaders. We follow preachers and pastors. We follow those who *lead*.

But let me share something important with you about spiritual leaders. They can lead you only as far as they can "see" with their faith. Leaders cannot enable you to "see" what they cannot "see" with their spiritual eyes. They cannot believe for something in your life that they don't believe for their own lives or take you to places they don't believe you can go.

Are you following a leader who helps you to see more than you can see? Are you following a leader who is helping you to hear more than you've heard about the power and greatness and provision and glory of God? Are you following someone who believes for more than you currently believe for? Are you following someone who can help you experience God in a way that's beyond what you've ever experienced?

Trust God to send you the right leader to lead you into your destiny. Ultimately, you don't *find* God's leader for your life. God *sends* that leader your way. Your role is not to *find* your leader. Your role is to *recognize* the leader that God sends, *invite* that leader into your life, and choose to *follow* that leader.

CONFRONT

1. What characteristics of a leader are important to God? _____

_____

_____

_____

_____

2. What are you seeing with your faith today? _____

_____

_____

_____

_____

3. If God has already sent a leader into your life, how can you follow better? If there is not a spiritual leader in your life, pray and ask God to send that person. _____

_____

_____

_____

_____

CONQUER

What do the Scriptures below mean to you personally and how can you apply them in your life?

Hebrews 13:7 _____

_____

_____

_____

1 Corinthians 11:1 _____

_____

_____

Hebrews 6:11, 12 _____

_____

_____

_____

DAY 2: EXAMINE YOUR ASSOCIATIONS

There are four types of people:

> People who add to your life
>
> People who subtract from your life
>
> People who multiply what God is doing in your life
>
> People who divide you from your God-given purpose in life

Make certain that you associate only with people who are adding and multiplying in your life, and that you withdraw from those who subtract or divide.

Withdraw from those God tells you to leave behind. Don't take into your future the people God tells you to leave in your past. Let them go! God is exceedingly wise, and He wants you to have strong, healthy, anointed relationships. He will lead you to those people who will encourage you in your walk with Him and affirm His destiny for your life and He will lead you away from those who won't. When He asks you to leave a relationship, start walking!

Withdraw from those who refuse spiritual authority. Because it is not good to be associated with rebellion or dishonor toward God's divine order, remove yourself from those who put themselves above or apart from spiritual authority. Even if you want to minister to such people, the best way to do that is to refrain from associating with them until they come under spiritual authority.

Withdraw from those who invite you to sin. The person who will sin *with* you will eventually sin *against* you—and sin has consequences. It steals, kills, or destroys something in you—it may be your innocence; it may be your reputation; it may be your health; it may be your emotional well-being. Sin will always get you in trouble and it always leads to death. Preserve your life, preserve your purity, and preserve your communion with God by running from sin and those who would tempt you to sin. Walk in what you know is right and enjoy God's blessing in your life!

CONFRONT

1. What relationships add or multiply in your life? _____

   _____

   _____

   _____

   _____

2. What relationships subtract or divide in your life? _____

   _____

   _____

   _____

   _____

3. How will you improve the relationships that add and multiply?
   How can you leave the ones that subtract and divide? _____

_____

_____

_____

_____

CONQUER

What do the Scriptures below mean to you personally and how can you apply them in your life?

Proverbs 13:20 _____

_____

_____

_____

Matthew 18:15–17 _____

_____

_____

_____

Romans 6:23 _____

_____

_____

_____

DAY 3: SEND THE RIGHT MESSAGE

We attract what we *think* we deserve. We constantly send off silent signals about the way we value ourselves. For example, a woman sends off silent signals in the way she walks, the way she holds her head, the way she dresses, and the way she comes into a room. She sends off signals in the way she talks and in the way she looks people in the eye. Her signals tell another person how she values herself.

If you believe you are to be the "head and not the tail," then you will walk as the "head" (see Deut. 28:13, NKJV). If you believe you are to be "above only, and not be beneath," then you will act in ways that send the message, "I'm blessed by God."

The problem with some people is that they don't believe they can ever be more than a seven-dollar-an-hour employee or that they can ever have enough money to pay their bills. Why? Because they don't believe they *deserve* to have money, and they don't respect the money they do have. Some people don't believe they can own their own companies. Why? Because they don't realize the value that is within them and not until they begin to value themselves can they begin to develop themselves.

People tell me they want more friends—but they don't respect and value the people who come their way who might become their friends.

People tell me they want more of God's anointing—but they don't respect the anointing they do have.

When you violate something good that God sends your way, God will not send you more of it! Anything you don't value, you violate. And what you don't value in yourself, others will also violate.

You can't really love another person unless you love yourself *first*. You won't value another person unless you value yourself first. Conversely, others won't love and value you unless you love and value yourself. They will respond to you the way *you* respond to yourself. When you love yourself, you attract other people to you who will value you for who you esteem yourself to be.

CONFRONT

1. How do you treat yourself? What signals are you sending others about your own worth and value? _____

   _____

   _____

   _____

   _____

2. Are you violating anything God has given you? How will you begin to value that instead? _____

_____

_____

_____

3. How can you express love to yourself and affirm your self-worth today?

_____

_____

_____

_____

CONQUER

What do the Scriptures below mean to you personally and how can you apply them in your life?

Matthew 22:39 _____

_____

_____

_____

Isaiah 43:4 _____

_____

_____

_____

James 1:17 _____

_____

_____

_____

DAY 4: DO'S AND DON'TS OF GOOD ASSOCIATIONS

Let me give you some "do's and don'ts" that will help you identify and develop good associations. I'll start with good associations with the leaders you choose to follow.

Don't follow people who are lazy.

Don't follow without direction or goals.

Don't follow people who are critical of those who prosper or when others are blessed.

Don't follow people who focus on the flaws of others.

Don't follow people who complain.

Don't follow people who act as though the world owes them something.

Don't follow people who see the problem and not the solution.

Do follow leaders who have a higher purpose—those who are following Christ no matter what happens.

Do follow leaders who are faithful in good times and bad.

Do follow leaders who rise above their circumstances to pursue a higher calling on their lives.

Do follow leaders who experience prosperity, which means wholeness and generosity in every area of life.

Do follow leaders who will help you see *clearly* what God has for you.

Generally, I encourage you to welcome the following types of people into your life, whether they are leaders or not:

Those who focus on your future, not on your past.

Those who believe your potential is unlimited.

Those who will call you out of your comfort zone and into a commitment zone.

Those who will encourage you.

CONFRONT

1. Ask God to help you develop discernment and wisdom as you choose to follow certain leaders and to keep you from following those He does not want you to associate with. _____

_____

_____

_____

_____

2. List several leaders who exhibit the good qualities mentioned in this lesson. How can you reap maximum benefit from their lives or ministries?

_____

_____

_____

_____

3. List several people who focus on your future, believe your potential is unlimited, call you to commitment, and encourage you. What can you do to strengthen your relationship with them? _____

_____

_____

_____

_____

CONQUER

What do the Scriptures below mean to you personally and how can you apply them in your life?

1 Corinthians 15:33 _____

_____

_____

_____

Proverbs 12:26 _____

_____

_____

_____

Romans 16:17, 18 _____

_____

_____

_____

DAY 5: FACE THE TRUTH

In this day's lesson, I want to share three key truths with you. Choose today to start listening only to those who walk in truth and speak the truth to you.

Truth #1: You have treasure *inside of you.* You need people in your life who can see the treasure inside you. The same God who stepped out on nothing and created everything, is the God who lives inside you. Paul wrote, "We have this treasure in earthen vessels" (2 Cor. 4:7, NKJV). You are not simply an earthen vessel—cracked, chipped, and easily broken. You have treasure inside you that is eternal, glorious, and beyond value. Choose friendships with people who appreciate that the Spirit of God lives within you and who value that you have treasure inside you!

Truth #2: You can achieve more than you've achieved, experience more than you have experienced, and have a greater anointing than you have. You need people who have achieved more than you have achieved, who know God better than you know God, who have experienced life beyond what you have experienced. You need people who have greater faith than you have, a greater understanding of God's Word than you have, a greater anointing than you have. You need to learn from them, to be encouraged by them, and to follow their examples.

Truth #3: You have Christ in you, working through you. All people have the same challenge and the same opportunity to release their full God-given potential. It begins with the truth of Galatians 2:20, which says, "I have been crucified with Christ; it is no longer I who live, but Christ lives in me; and the life which I now live in the flesh I live by faith in the Son of God, who loved me and gave Himself for me" (NKJV). When Christ lives in you and you live by faith in Him, you can do everything He asks of you by the strength He imparts to you.

Choose to believe the truth that Christ dwells in you, loves you, and gave Himself for you. He wants to live His life in you and through you to touch others. When you develop the gift of God in you, you become a world changer and a history maker!

CONFRONT

1. Is there any area of your life in which you are not believing God's truth? How can you combat that with the truth of the Word?

_____

_____

_____

_____

2. What would you like to achieve that you haven't yet achieved? What would you like to experience that you haven't yet experienced?

_____

_____

_____

_____

3. List some practical ways you can express the truth that Christ lives in you. _____

_____

_____

_____

_____

CONQUER

What do the Scriptures below mean to you personally and how can you apply them in your life?

John 17:17 _____

_____

_____

_____

John 8:32 _____

_____

_____

_____

1 Corinthians 6:19 _____

_____

_____

_____

Lesson 9

THE DAUGHTERS OF ZELOPHEHAD:
Dealing with What Belongs to You

To learn more about the Daughters of Zelophehad, read Numbers 27:1–7 and Chapter 9 of the book, *Deal with It!*

DAY 1: DON'T SETTLE FOR LESS

Many of God's people are bored and apathetic. They haven't challenged what life has handed to them. They haven't tried to move into their God-given potential or learned to exercise their gifts. They haven't acted on the truths of God's Word or begun to release the power God has put in them. Even though deep inside they may want more, they have ended up frustrated because they have settled for less than their God-appointed destiny.

We all have a tendency to settle for "less"—it's human nature to want to let things be and not to work hard or challenge the status quo. It takes effort to prepare for a better future and it takes courage to step out of our comfort zones. But, God always calls us beyond our comfort zones. He always challenges us to do more, be more, and take on more. He challenges us to trust Him and then to act on our faith. He always calls us to stop settling for less.

When Jesus said, "It is finished," He was declaring that He had given all there was to give and done everything He needed to do for us. He had given us His life and made provision for us to receive the Holy Spirit. He had purchased all of the health and forgiveness and blessing we could ever receive and use. He had done "more than enough" for our deliverance, protection, provision, peace, and restoration. We don't need anything more than we have already been given; we simply need to learn how to walk in what has been accomplished on our behalf and released to us! We must receive all that Jesus purchased for us by His death and resurrection and live in the fullness of the victory He has given us!

CONFRONT

1. Are you suffering from boredom or apathy in any way? If so, how can you challenge yourself to overcome that? _____

_____

_____

_____

_____

2. In what ways are you settling for less? How can you break out of that comfort zone? _____

_____

_____

_____

_____

3. Starting today, how can you practically live in the victory Jesus has given you? _____

_____

_____

_____

_____

CONQUER

What do the Scriptures below mean to you personally and how can you apply them in your life?

1 John 4:4 _____

_____

_____

_____

Romans 8:11 _____

_____

_____

_____

2 Peter 1:3 _____

_____

_____

_____

DAY 2: LIVE UNTIL YOU DIE

James 4:14 says, "For what is your life? It is even a vapor that appears for a little time and then vanishes away" (NKJV). Go into any cemetery and on the gravestones, below the names of people who have died, you will see two dates—their birth date and their date of death—with a hyphen between the dates. The most important part of that person's life, however, does not lie in those dates. It lies in what happened in the hyphen! Ultimately, what's going to matter is the quality of life you live, the character you develop, and the legacy you leave.

What a shame to die without ever living! God has a purpose for you every morning that you wake up on this earth. Every time you open your eyes and open your mouth, God has a purpose for what you see and what you say.

Great songs, great books, great sermons, great businesses, great acts of love and kindness, great deeds of heroism, and great witnesses for the gospel of Jesus Christ are buried in graveyards—having died without ever being expressed or established. Dreams come to pass when you *work* your dreams and your potential, when you step out and challenge life and take on the possibilities before you. If you are just sitting around thinking or talking about your dreams and your potential, you will never move into your destiny; you will accomplish *nothing* and your dreams will die with you.

Your heavenly Father has made provision for you. He is waiting to escort you into your destiny. You are the only one who can keep your dreams alive and cause them to become realities. Don't let them be buried with you. Get busy and live them!

CONFRONT

1. What are you doing today to make your life matter, to make it count for something, to live a life of importance and influence? _____

   _____

   _____

   _____

   _____

2. In what way today can you step out and demonstrate your faith in God to bring your dreams to pass? _____

   _____

   _____

   _____

   _____

3. What specific dream(s) in your heart will you commit to seeing fulfilled, no matter what? _____

   _____

   _____

   _____

   _____

CONQUER

What do the Scriptures below mean to you personally and how can you apply them in your life?

John 10:10 _____

_____

_____

_____

Ecclesiastes 5:3 _____

_____

_____

_____

Philippians 4:13 _____

_____

_____

_____

DAY 3: DEFEATING DISCRIMINATION

To *discriminate* means to "differentiate," to treat somebody with prejudice (which is a preconceived judgment). It means to judge a person as "different" for some reason—ethnically, socioeconomically, or in gender, age, belief, life experience, or some other reason—and therefore, as inferior.

It's one thing to accept your unique qualities and your "differences." It's another thing to be discriminated against because you are unique or "different."

Discrimination is rooted in jealousy and fear, and it hurts because it includes rejection. *Rejection* means to "deny" or "to refuse to acknowledge" or to "cast or throw aside as being useless." A person who is rejected feels devalued and less worthy than others.

But, if a person doesn't *need* the approval of other people, that person rarely feels rejection or the negative feelings associated with discrimination. The only way to *not* feel a need for other people's approval is to know deep inside yourself that God totally accepts you and approves of you. You can survive discrimination if you know who you are in Christ.

Recognize that people who deny you, refuse to acknowledge you, or reject you don't have the ability to see the real you. Only God has the ability to see all of you, from your beginning all the way to your ending, from your imperfection all the way to your perfection, and from where you are right now all the way to where you are going to be one day. Only God knows you completely, and on the basis of the full information He has about you, He says that you are "more" (see Rom. 8:37).

That's why God's opinion is the *only* opinion that really counts! That's why it's critically important that you know what God thinks of you. You need to recognize that He has already accepted you fully and that He values you more highly than you could ever imagine.

CONFRONT

1. Have you ever suffered discrimination? On what basis? _____

   _____

   _____

   _____

   _____

2. How could what makes you "different" to some people be useful in the hands of the Lord? _____

   _____

   _____

   _____

   _____

3. Pray and ask God what He says when He sees the real you. Write down your impressions after you pray. _____

   _____

   _____

   _____

   _____

CONQUER

What do the Scriptures below mean to you personally and how can you apply them in your life?

Psalm 33:15 _____

_____

_____

_____

Ephesians 1:6 _____

_____

_____

_____

Psalm 139:14 _____

_____

_____

_____

DAY 4: EXERCISE THE POWER OF A REQUEST

James 4:2 says, "You do not have because you do not ask" (NKJV). There is tremendous power in a request—and the daughters of Zelophehad knew it! A person who knows what to ask, when to ask, and how to ask is difficult to refuse.

There is a way to challenge any system by making a request, and there is a way to make a request without violating principles or dishonoring those you approach. You are not to make requests in anger or bitterness, or with unforgiveness, doubt, or anxiety (see Phil. 4:6 and James 1:6–8). You are to make your requests with boldness, love, wisdom and kindness.

One key to making a request is to know *your* inheritance. You need to know what God has promised *you*. Your inheritance includes: the promises God makes to *all* those who know Jesus as their Savior and follow Him as their Lord; the promises God makes to all who keep His commandments and who meditate on and speak His Word; and the promises God has spoken to your own heart—things that are specifically for *you*.

One way you can know those things that are specifically for you is to find confirmation in God's Word. Another way is by paying attention as God speaks to your heart while you are praying about the matter.

Go to God's Word and ask the Lord, "What are my rights? What is it You have for *me?* What is *my* inheritance?"

If God promises you peace, don't settle for worry and stress.

If God promises you renewed strength and joy, don't settle for exhaustion and frustration.

If God promises you godly relationships, don't settle for ungodly alliances.

Go to God's Word and ask Him, "What do You have for me?" Pray and listen for Him to answer. When He speaks to your heart, act on His response. Claim your inheritance!

CONFRONT

1. What are some of the things God has promised to all believers?

   _____

   _____

   _____

   _____

2. What do you believe are some of God's specific promises to you? How have those things been confirmed through your reading of the Word and through prayer? _____

   _____

   _____

   _____

3. Based on what you know of your inheritance, what should you be requesting that you have not yet asked for? _____

_____

_____

_____

_____

CONQUER

What do the Scriptures below mean to you personally and how can you apply them in your life?

Hebrews 4:16 _____

_____

_____

Matthew 21:22 _____

_____

_____

Luke 11:9 _____

_____

_____

DAY 5: PURSUE YOUR PASSION

The dream and passion in your heart is a major part of God's inheritance for you, and the pursuit of that dream and passion will bring great fulfillment to your life.

If you dread getting up and going to work on Monday morning, ask yourself, "Why am I working this job?" Find a job that you can hardly wait to get to! There are plenty of jobs in this world, plenty of ways to make money. Pursue your *God-given* passion as your first priority.

You may need to downsize some of the trappings of your life as you make the transition to the pursuit of your passion and dream. Consider that a temporary season. It *will* be temporary and the rewards *will* be rich, and I assure you that the results will be worth the sacrifice!

Take a new look at how you are spending your time and resources. Are you building something? Are you willing to sacrifice today for the tomorrow you know God has planned for you? Are you willing to give now so you can receive later?

Don't live your life to fulfill the expectations or desires of another person. Live your life in pursuit of the dream God has planted in your heart—a dream only *you* can pursue and only *you* can fulfill.

Instead of accepting the limits that have been placed on you—including the limits you have placed on yourself—challenge the system and pursue your passion!

Instead of accepting the way it's always been done, challenge the system and pursue your passion!

Instead of settling for less than you know is rightfully yours before God—challenge the system and pursue your passion!

CONFRONT

1. What is your dream—your true passion? _____

   _____

   _____

   _____

   _____

2. Are you pursuing *your* God-given passion and destiny? If not, what is one specific, practical step you can take in that direction?

   _____

   _____

   _____

   _____

3. Are you experiencing the fulfillment and success that is part of your inheritance? If not, what changes do you need to make in order to begin doing so? _____

_____

_____

_____

_____

CONQUER

What do the Scriptures below mean to you personally and how can you apply them in your life?

Ecclesiastes 5:18 _____

_____

_____

_____

Psalm 90:17 _____

_____

_____

_____

Psalm 37:4 _____

_____

_____

_____

Lesson 10

ESTHER:
Dealing with Destiny

To understand who Esther was and the challenges she faced, read Esther 4:13, 14 and Chapter 10 of the book, *Deal With It!*

DAY 1: EMBRACE YOUR CRISIS

Esther was an extraordinary woman. To be extraordinary means to be great, out of the box, beyond the norm. A woman who is extraordinary is great for God and aware of His purpose and destiny for her life.

The extraordinary woman named Esther found herself in a crisis, and I need to tell you that just because someone is extraordinary doesn't mean that she can't experience a crisis. In fact, crisis is likely to come because crisis develops character.

A crisis is a turning point; a moment of decision. It is the decisive time when a situation reaches the point of being critical. Crises occur when the future is at stake. That's the situation in which Esther found herself.

Millions of people today are in crisis on any given day. They may experience a crisis at home, when they discovered that the child they raised to be a godly person is now smoking pot or when the husband to whom they have been faithful for decades comes home smelling like another woman's cologne. They may face a crisis at work when the job they have done well for years is being "phased out." They may face a health crisis, a financial crisis, or an emotional crisis.

The question posed to Esther in her moment of crisis is a powerful one: "Who knows whether you have come to the kingdom for such a time as this?"

If you are experiencing a crisis today, could it be that your crisis is a catalyst for a greater role or position? Could it be that your "pit" is preparing you for the "palace"? Could it be God is positioning *you* for a greater purpose?

Who knows, like Esther, you may have come to God's kingdom for such a time as this!

CONFRONT

1. What has been the most difficult crisis of your life? _____

    _____

    _____

    _____

    _____

2. How did your crisis build your character? _____

    _____

    _____

    _____

    _____

3. How do you think God can use the lessons and character development that resulted from your crisis in His kingdom? _____

    _____

    _____

    _____

    _____

CONQUER

What do the Scriptures below mean to you personally and how can you apply them in your life?

James 1:2–4 _____

_____

_____

_____

1 Peter 4:12, 13 _____

_____

_____

_____

Psalm 20:4 _____

_____

_____

_____

DAY 2: SUSTAINED FOR GOD'S PURPOSE

Have you been abused and misused, forsaken and forgotten, broken and battered? If so, the truth is that God has sustained you through it all and brought you to this point. You haven't arrived where you are today by your great ability, education, family background, social position, intellect, beauty, skills, or sheer willpower. You are where you are today because God has sustained you.

Our amazing God with His amazing grace has sustained you for His purposes. He has saved you, given you a testimony, called you, and raised you up for this very moment, this very opportunity, this very challenge!

He is your strength! God's Word says, "My God shall be My strength" (Is. 49:5, NKJV).

He is your refuge! God's Word says the Lord is "my strength and my fortress, my refuge in the day of affliction" (Jer. 16:19, NKJV).

He is your rock and defender! The Bible says, "He only is my rock and my salvation; He is my defense; I shall not be greatly moved" (Ps. 62:2, NKJV).

You are who you are and where you are because of Him. When you know that God has sustained you thus far and that He has *more* for you in your future than anything in your yesterday, then you have the strength to persevere through any crisis and to live in the anticipation that your greater blessing is on its way!

Anytime you think you might not make it, remind yourself of the truth and the promises of God's Word. Your strength comes from God—it's not something you can work up in yourself. You can do all things *through Christ*. It is God's strength poured into you and working through you that enables you to overcome, to persevere, and to be strong.

CONFRONT

1. What are some specific ways God has sustained you in the past?

   _____

   _____

   _____

   _____

2. How can you actively live in anticipation of the blessing you desire?

   _____

   _____

   _____

   _____

3. Memorize and meditate on one of the Bible verses listed in this lesson or in "Work the Word" below. Allow that Scripture to strengthen you as you move toward accomplishing God's purposes for your life.

   _____

   _____

   _____

   _____

CONQUER

What do the Scriptures below mean to you personally and how can you apply them in your life?

Romans 8:37 _____

_____

_____

_____

2 Corinthians 2:14 _____

_____

_____

_____

1 John 5:4 _____

_____

_____

_____

DAY 3: HOW TO BE EXTRAORDINARY, PART 1

Let's explore the qualities that made Esther extraordinary because they will help you accomplish God's purpose for your life.

1. *Be broken, but not bitter.* We all experience some brokenness in life, but we do not have to become bitter. Instead, we are to allow God to restore us with His love, His grace, and His healing touch.

Life can deplete you. It saps your strength, drains your creativity, silences your enthusiasm, siphons off your resources. But God offers restoration and gives purpose to your pain. When God restores you, He makes you whole. He fills you with purpose and determination instead of questions and doubts. He gives you the courage to love again, to face fear, and to experience life fully.

God wants to restore those areas that have been fragmented, ripped, and raped in your life. Allow His love to pierce your pain, heal you, restore your sense of purpose, and make you whole. Refuse to be bitter over your brokenness. Let God's love *restore you!*

2. *Be submitted to authority.* Esther was independent yet submissive. There is safety, freedom, and protection in submission. Submission is part of God's order; it ensures that you can be productive and successful in life.

Order is the accurate, effective, and productive arrangement of things. If you are out of order—if you seek to get out from under proper authority—chaos results. But when you stay under authority, blessings result.

3. *Develop the inner confidence to handle pressure.* Pressure is not necessarily bad. Pressure can make you produce. The challenge of pressure is learning how to handle it—which requires developing internal confidence and inner strength. Devote your time and energy to building yourself up from the inside out. Come to the awareness that God is in you. Believe what He says you are and will be and will do, so that you will be strong enough to handle the pressures you face on your way to your destiny!

CONFRONT

1. Has your brokenness made you bitter? If so, ask God to restore you.

   _____

   _____

   _____

   _____

2. Are you properly submitted to authority? If not, what adjustments do you need to make? _____

   _____

   _____

   _____

   _____

3. In what ways can you develop the inner confidence and strength needed to handle pressure? _____

   _____

   _____

   _____

CONQUER

What do the Scriptures below mean to you personally and how can you apply them in your life?

Psalm 23:3 _____

_____

_____

_____

Romans 13:1 _____

_____

_____

_____

Romans 5:3, 4 _____

_____

_____

_____

DAY 4: HOW TO BE EXTRAORDINARY, PART 2

Let's continue looking at the qualities that make a person extraordinary.

4. *Be willing to undergo the process of preparation.* Preparation is the process that begins with a promise and ends with full provision. It is a series of actions that lead to a determined end or destiny.

The process of preparation is just that—a *process.* God does not refine, train, transform, or renew you instantly. He puts you through a *process*—and that requires patience, perseverance, steadfastness, faithfulness, ongoing trust, and radical obedience to His Word.

5. *Seek God's wisdom.* Wisdom is knowing what to say and when to say it. It is the comprehensive insight into the ways and purposes of God. Knowledge comes from study, but wisdom comes from God. We all need more of God's wisdom, and His Word promises that He will give it if we will ask. Only God can give you the insight and understanding about how to walk in *His* ways and accomplish *His* destiny for your life.

6. *Get the necessary information.* Be aware of your surroundings and know what is going on in your sphere of influence. If you are called to minister to your neighborhood, know your neighborhood. If you are called to influence the business community for God, know how to conduct yourself in the business world. If you are called to intercede for your government, know your leaders and the issues they are dealing with. Educate yourself, because information empowers you to make quality decisions.

7. *Be troubled by the troubles of others to the point of action.* Be a person who responds to suffering with compassion, and associate with people who are troubled by the troubles of others and who move to help them. When you see a need, reach out to meet it. As you obey God by caring for others, you will position yourself to receive what God has to meet *your* needs.

CONFRONT

1. How can you better cooperate with God's process of preparation in your life? _____

_____

_____

_____

2. In what areas of your life or ministry do you need to get more information? _____

_____

_____

_____

3. How can you be more proactive in responding to the suffering around you? _____

_____

_____

_____

CONQUER

What do the Scriptures below mean to you personally and how can you apply them in your life?

Hebrews 12:11 _____

_____

_____

_____

James 1:5 _____

_____

_____

_____

Proverbs 31:8, 9 _____

_____

_____

_____

DAY 5: DON'T MISS YOUR MOMENT

Why develop the seven qualities listed in Day 3 and 4? Why choose to become *extraordinary?* Because God has something extraordinary for you to do!

Everything you have gone through in your life has brought you to *this* moment so you might change your world and influence people for God.

Where there is torment—you are to bring God's peace.

Where there is confusion—you are to bring God's wisdom and truth in clarity.

Where there is hell—you are to bring the message and hope of heaven.

Are you wondering about your purpose? Are you wondering why certain things have happened to you in the past or are happening to you today? God is preparing you! He is transforming you into a person who will rise above bitterness and overflow with His love. He is transforming you into a person who is independent and strong, yet submissive to His authority at all times. He is establishing in you the ability to withstand pressure and giving you the inner confidence that comes from a relationship with Him.

God's desire today is to bring relief and deliverance to His people, just as it was in Esther's day. But will that relief and deliverance come through *you*? Will you have anything to do with the healing that God desires to bring to a person who is sick physically, emotionally, mentally, or spiritually? Will you have a part in meeting the needs that God desires to meet? Will you win the souls that God desires to be won? Will you be the one who speaks what God desires to be spoken?

Your life is bursting with promise and potential; your future is bathed in the glory of God; and your destiny is worth pursuing with your whole heart.

CONFRONT

1. Do you have any doubts about God's destiny for your life? Ask Him to reveal His purposes for you and to give you a glimpse of the future He has already prepared for you. _____

_____

_____

_____

2. Briefly describe how you believe everything you have gone through has prepared you for your destiny. _____

_____

_____

_____

3. Practically, how will you pursue your destiny with all of your heart? Specifically, what will you do? _____

_____

_____

_____

_____

CONQUER

What do the Scriptures below mean to you personally and how can you apply them in your life?

Esther 4:14b _____

_____

_____

_____

Colossians 3:23 _____

_____

_____

_____

2 Thessalonians 1:11, 12 _____

_____

_____

_____

ABOUT
THE AUTHOR

PAULA WHITE, pastor, teacher, and speaker, is known for her dynamic Bible teaching and preaching with delivery as an exhorter and motivator. She is also the host of the nationally syndicated program, *Paula White Today*, seen on BET, TBN, Church Channel, Word Network, Court TV, Miracle Network, and Daystar Television Network, as well as many other stations. With a message that crosses denominational, cultural, and economic barriers, this wife, mother, preacher, administrator, humanitarian, and evangelist is also the Co-Pastor and Co-Founder of Without Walls International Church. Together with her husband, Dr. Randy White, they pastor a thriving, multi-racial congregation of some 15,000 in Tampa, Florida, one of the fastest growing churches of its kind in the country.

BIRTHING YOUR DREAMS

ISBN: 0-7852-5069-7

Birthing Your Dreams guides women through the process of identifying their dreams, focusing on goals while maintaining balance in their lives, and finally realizing the fruit of their labors. A recurring theme to Paula's message is for women to "PUSH!"

- PUSH negativity and doubts from your mind.
- PUSH sin in action from your heart.
- PUSH people who don't serve God from your life.
- PUSH God into the center of your existence.
- PUSH to have your voice heard. PUSH your dreams to reality.

There are obstacles standing in the way of a woman who wants to fulfill her dreams and leaving these obstacles behind is a struggle and labor of love. Paula White, pastor of Without Walls International Church in Tampa, Florida, is a world-renowned speaker who addresses thousands of women every year. Her spiritual gift is coaching hurting women through the dream-birthing process.

NELSON REFERENCE & ELECTRONIC
A Division of Thomas Nelson Publishers
Since 1798
www.thomasnelson.com

ISBN: 0-7852-6106-0

DEAL
WITH IT!

This is a book that dares to go where others have not—addressing the real issues that modern women face. Nobody understands the issues women face better than dynamic Bible teacher and national speaker Paula White, host of a national television program, who crosses multiracial and gender lines with her messages. Many of these listeners are women who identify with Paula's straight-forward and candid approach as she shares from what she has experienced in life. Her openness, integrity, and honesty are what draw men and women to her. In this book, Paula highlights 10 women in the Bible and shows how God transformed their lives and can transform anyone's life who is seeking Him and the answers he provides throughout Scripture.

NELSON BOOKS
A Division of Thomas Nelson Publishers
Since 1798

www.thomasnelson.com